MANDALA
SOURCEBOOK

MANDALA
SOURCEBOOK

150 MANDALAS TO HELP YOU FIND PEACE, AWARENESS & WELL-BEING

DAVID FONTANA
&
LISA TENZIN-DOLMA

FAIR WINDS
PRESS
BEVERLY, MASSACHUSETTS

In memory of David Fontana
(1934–2010)

Mandala Sourcebook

First published in the USA in 2014 by
Fair Winds Press, a member of
Quayside Publishing Group
100 Cummings Center
Suite 406-L
Beverly, Massachusetts 01915-6101
www.fairwindspress.com

Original material taken from *Healing Mandalas*,
Natural Mandalas and *Meditating with Mandalas*,
published by Watkins Publishing Limited

18 17 16 15 14   1 2 3 4 5

ISBN 978-1-59233-616-6

Typeset in Bembo
Colour reproduction by PDQ, UK
Printed in China

The information in this book is for educational
purposes only. It is not intended to replace the
advice of a physician or medical practitioner.
Please see your health care provider before
beginning any new health program.
that are mentioned herein.

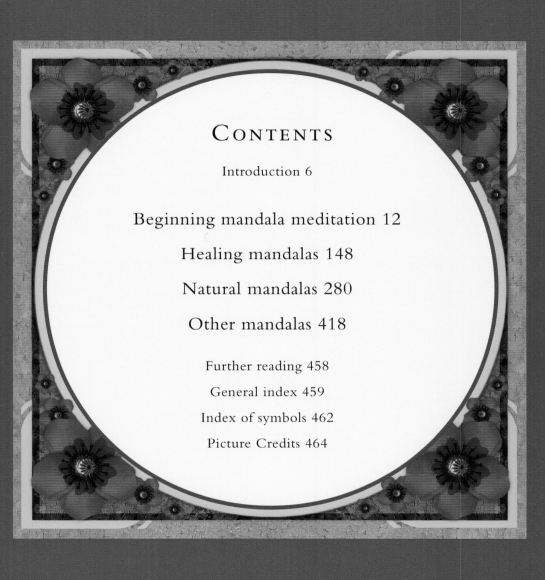

Contents

The World of Mandalas

MANDALAS ARE SYMBOLIC PICTURES USED IN MEDITATION.
IMPORTANT IN MOST EASTERN TRADITIONS, THEY TAKE
THE MEDITATOR ON A WORDLESS JOURNEY INTO THE
MIND'S DEEPEST MYSTERIES.

Mandalas are probably as old as humankind itself. In rudimentary form they appear on walls and in caves in some of the earliest marks made by humans, and they are present again in some of the first scribbles of young children. They express through symbolism something innate in ourselves. Like all true symbols they arise from deep levels of the unconscious, and as such serve as keys which can take us into the mysterious recesses of our own minds.

THE ETERNAL CIRCLE

The most basic of all mandalas is the circle, an important and universal symbol to which the human psyche responds at the very deepest level. It is the still centre of the turning world, the magic enclosure that defines and protects a sacred space within which one finds tranquillity and peace. It is the wheel of life, the symbol of ultimate perfection, the tunnel between this world and the world to come, the promise of eternity.

The circle of the mandala is a primal symbol for all that exists. It is the symbol of the sun, the giver of light, and of the full moon, the discloser of dark mysteries.

Totality, perfection, unity, eternity
– the circle is a symbol of completeness
that can include ideas of both
permanence and dynamism. Apart from
the point or centre with which it shares
much of its symbolism, the circle is the
only geometric shape without divisions
and alike at all points. Because the circle,
which can also represent a sphere, is
a form potentially without beginning
or end, it is the most resonant of all
geometric symbols in the traditions of
mystical thought.

THE MANDALA TRADITION

Not only is the circle the most basic
of all mandalas, it is the form upon
which all mandalas are based – the
word "mandala" is in fact the Sanskrit
word for "disk". Although the circle
may contain other shapes within it,

such as the square and the triangle, and
sometimes may even be bounded on the
outside by one or other of these shapes,
the circle remains the primary feature
of all mandalas. Without the circle, there
is no mandala. But once the circle is
drawn, then other symbols can be added
to it. These more complex mandalas
are major features of the sacred art of
many spiritual traditions, particularly
of Hinduism and Buddhism. At their
most complete, these elaborate mandalas
constitute symbolic pictures of the
cosmos, replete either with the divine
beings who represent or embody the
cosmic forces behind existence, or with
the geometrical shapes that signify these
forces in more abstract form – the term
"yantra" is sometimes used for these
purely geometrical mandalas.

In the spiritual traditions, the
mandala is frequently used as an aid

to meditation. Because of its symbolic nature, the mandala when used in this way can help the mind not only to become focused and tranquil, but also to access progressively deeper levels of the unconscious, ultimately assisting the meditator to experience a mystical sense of oneness with the ultimate unity from which the cosmos in all its manifold forms arises.

MANDALAS WORLDWIDE

Although mandalas are particularly associated with the East, they have in fact been an important feature of Western traditions as well. In Christianity one of the best-known examples is the Celtic cross, in which the centre of the circle is also the centre of the cross, whose four arms then extend beyond the circumference to symbolize, among other things, the four dimensions, the human form, and the link between the heavens above and the Earth below (see page 44). In fact, the symbol probably predates Christianity. We sometimes see the cross contained fully within the circle, while at other times it is much smaller and takes the form of the rose, as in the "rosy cross" of the Rosicrucians (see page 108). There are also echoes of the mandala in the halo that surrounds the head of Christ and the saints in Christian art.

In Islam, which forbids the portrayal of Allah or of Muhammad, geometrical shapes dominate sacred art and architecture, and a segment of the circle, the crescent, together with the full circle in the form of a star, represent the divine. The inverted half circle, the dome, represents the arch of the heavens and, by forming the roof of the mosque, allows the whole building to become a three-dimensional mandala, helping to turn the minds of the faithful toward Allah.

In Hinduism, Buddhism and Jainism, the three great traditions that originated in India, the mandala is an integral part of sacred art and a central feature of many meditational practices. The ground plan of the Hindu temple often takes the form of a mandala symbolizing the universe, with doors or gates at each of the cardinal points. Sometimes colours are associated with each of these points – yellow for north, red for east, black for south and white for west – while the centre, the point at which all four meet and from which all four arise, is green, the hue of creation. In the East the lotus is sacred not only because its flower transcends the darkness of the water and of the mud where it has its roots,

but also because its symmetrical petals make a perfect mandala. In Buddhism the mandala is an essential feature of the Tibetan tradition, in some of its more elaborate forms representing a mystical journey that takes the meditator from ignorance to enlightenment.

In the West the circular maze, such as the one on the floor of Chartres Cathedral in northern France, is another representation of the symbolic journey from outer darkness to the sacred centre of the spirit, where the individual soul finds itself in the presence of the divine.

Meditators in the West today tend to favour mandalas that are universal, rather than mythic, in their symbolism. Certain ingredients, such as the lotus and river, have a broad symbolic appeal; whereas the wrathful deities of the Tibetan mandala can be too esoteric for non-specialized use.

WORKING WITH
THIS BOOK

Resist the temptation to flick through this book, glancing at one mandala after another without really taking them in. This doesn't mean that you must work with each of them before you can go on to the next. By all means look through the book – probably you will do so anyway – but keep in mind that you are not simply looking at pretty pictures. The mandalas are very much more than that. They each have a symbolic life of their own, and coming to know them will take time and practice, just as it takes time to come to know new friends.

There are 150 mandalas in the book grouped in four sections: Beginning Mandala Meditation, Healing Mandalas, Natural Mandalas and Other Mandalas. It is hoped that these categories are self-explanatory, but there is inevitably, of course, a great deal of overlap: given that the overall aim is holistic, it would have been counterproductive to insist on divisions. Avoid thinking of the mandalas as forming a sequence from easy to difficult. Each mandala is complete in itself. There is no hierarchy between them. Some are based on traditional Tibetan mandalas, while others are inspired by nature or symbols found in various cultures.

When selecting a new mandala on which to meditate, you can make your choice on a purely visual basis, choosing the one that appeals to you most at the time. Alternatively, you might base your selection on the mandalas' symbols: the step-by-step text alongside each mandala is ideal for anyone who feels daunted by the thought of approaching the images without specific guidance.

BEGINNING MANDALA MEDITATION

INTENSELY VISUAL AND FRAMED WITHIN A DYNAMIC DESIGN, MANDALAS ARE A POWERFUL TOOL FOR MEDITATION. THE STEP-BY-STEP GUIDELINES ALONGSIDE EACH IMAGE IN THIS SECTION ARE INTENDED TO INTRODUCE THE BEGINNER TO SOME OF THE THINKING BEHIND THE MEDITATION. AS YOUR MEDITATIVE PRACTICE DEVELOPS, THESE GUIDELINES CAN BE LEFT BEHIND, ALLOWING THE MANDALAS TO WORK AT AN INCREASINGLY INTUITIVE AND PERSONAL LEVEL. ALTHOUGH THE MANDALAS ARE ORGANIZED BY THEME FOR EASE OF REFERENCE, YOUR EXPERIENCE OF ANY OF THE MANDALAS IS VERY MUCH YOUR OWN. ALL THE MANDALAS ARE, AT THE DEEPEST LEVEL, A REFLECTION OF THE SELF, THE COSMOS AND THE LOVE THAT BINDS EVERYTHING TOGETHER.

*Mandalas are symbolic pictures used in meditation.
Important in most Eastern traditions, they take the
meditator on a wordless journey into the mind's
deepest mysteries.*

*The most basic of all mandalas is the circle, an intriguing
symbol that has no beginning and no end. ... It is the still
centre of the turning world, the magic circle that defines
and protects a sacred space within which one finds
tranquillity and peace.*

*It is the wheel of life, the symbol of ultimate perfection,
the tunnel between this world and the world to come,
the symbol of eternity.*

MANDALAS AND MEDITATION

Meditation is a practice for calming the mind. Usually our minds are so dominated by what is going on around us or by our own mental chatter that we have little opportunity to experience the peaceful, tranquil state that is the natural condition of the mind. So habitual does this domination become that we take it for granted. If we are asked to stop thinking for one minute, most of us would be unable to do so. In a very real sense, our minds are not our own. They are so distracted first by one thing, then another, and so pulled this way and that by sensations, thoughts, memories and emotions and by the demands of the outer world that we have very little control over them.

WHY MEDITATE?

Meditation is a path of self-discovery. We may think that we know ourselves, but in fact we live mostly in our conscious minds, and remain unaware of the depths of our unconscious and of the subtle spiritual dimension of our own being. By helping to still the train of thoughts that dominates the conscious mind, meditation opens us to the deeper mysteries of our inner selves.

The results of such a boost in mental power can be seen on an everyday level. By increasing our ability to concentrate, meditation can aid memory and make us more alert to the world around us. It also has potential physical benefits: it helps to relax the body and combat the effects of stress. There is evidence that for some people meditation may help to lower blood pressure, assist with pain management and promote restful, restorative sleep.

The result is that we live much of our waking lives in a state of tension; and when the mind becomes tense, so does the body. Mind and body are so intrinsically linked that many of our physical ailments are a consequence, directly or indirectly, of what goes on inside our heads.

Meditation helps the mind to learn to become focused upon just one stimulus, and to cease to attend to all the distractions competing for our attention. The stimulus may be our breathing, or it may be a mantra (a sacred sound or phrase) or a mandala. If we use our breathing, we simply place our awareness upon the subtle sensation at the base of the nostrils as we breathe in and out. If we voice a mantra, we repeat it over and over to ourselves. And if we select a mandala, we place our gaze softly and attentively upon the image. In each case,

whenever our thoughts begin to stray, we bring them gently but firmly back to the point of focus. We do not force ourselves to stop thinking. Thoughts will inevitably arise, particularly when we are beginning to learn meditation or when we have had a busy or fretful day, but when they do so we simply refrain from attending to them and do not allow them to take control of our minds.

Because vision has always been such an important part of human experience, the mandala has proved over the centuries to be a particularly helpful point of focus in meditation. It can often hold our attention more effectively than non-visual stimuli. A mandala also has the added advantage that, provided it is a true mandala, its symbolic content will take us, without our having to make any special effort, into that inner world that lies at the heart of meditation.

In the Zen garden one of the aims is to capture the essence of a natural object, just as meditation allows us to experience that quiet, tranquil state at the core of our being.

STARTING MEDITATION

When you begin meditating with mandalas, even if you have practised meditation before, it is best to start with accessible designs, such as the ones contained in this book. The traditional, elaborate mandalas used in much of Tibetan Buddhism can and should be used only under detailed instructions from a lama who has himself been initiated into the spiritual practices that they represent. Use of these mandalas by the uninitiated is unlikely to do much good. The meditator can all too easily become distracted by the strength of the images and the vibrancy of the colours, and by the multitude of questions that they are likely to arouse in his or her mind. Like a secret code, to which the meditator does not have the key, the mandala will refuse to reveal its secrets. Instead, it is better to begin with something more simple, commencing if you wish with geometrical shapes.

Geometrical shapes have an archetypal force in that they are part of our inherited psyche, representing the patterns of the natural world within our minds. The mystery schools of ancient Greece, particularly that of Pythagoras, made a special study of geometry for this reason, and many of the sacred sites of the ancient world, such as the pyramids of Egypt and South America, and the stone circles of Western Europe, such as those at Stonehenge, Carnac and Avebury, were constructed to conform to what is known as "sacred geometry", which reproduced through man-made objects the patterns upon which this world, the heavens and the cosmos itself were thought to have been constructed.

MANDALA MEDITATION STEP BY STEP

Meditation is at one and the same time disarmingly simple yet challengingly difficult. Simple because the basic principles are readily learned, but difficult because the mind stubbornly refuses to keep to them. The secret is patience and practice. Meditation is not learnt in a few days. But if you remain patient with yourself and practise regularly, progress will come.

1 Find a quiet room where you won't be disturbed. Sit cross-legged on a firm cushion that raises your bottom a little way above the floor or sit in an upright chair with your feet flat on the floor.

2 Place the mandala you have chosen at eye level about an arm's length, or slightly more, in front of you. Start with a basic pattern such as a Celtic Cross (see page 44). Straighten your back and rest your hands in your lap, fingers laced together and palms uppermost.

3 Now rest your gaze on the mandala but relax your eye muscles. If your eyes go into soft focus so that you can see two images of the mandala instead of one, no matter. Blink only as often as necessary. Remain focused on the image. Do not be distracted by any thoughts that arise. If your attention wanders, bring it back each time to the mandala. Try not to think about the mandala. Simply look at it, steadily and evenly.

4 To begin with, practise for five minutes each day. If before five minutes are up you begin to feel disturbed in any way by the visual nature of the experience (see page 28), draw the meditation to a close. Remain always within the time limit in which you feel comfortable. As you become used to this form of meditation, you can extend this time limit, until ultimately you may be sitting for a full 20 or 30 minutes at each session. But never try to rush things or to push yourself too hard.

If you start with a mandala based on a geometrical shape such as a Celtic Cross (see page 44), you will find that early in your meditation a number of its symbolic meanings will arise unbidden in your mind. Without forcing it, simply allow this to happen. Note these meanings, without judgment, as they arise. Note how they seem to emerge of themselves from some deep level of your unconscious. But do not be tempted to try to commit them to memory. You can ponder their significance after the meditation is over.

STILLING BODY AND MIND

The essence of meditation is stillness. Unless you are following various practices of the Jain tradition (one of the great spiritual traditions of India), which are performed while standing, or doing a walking meditation (*kinhin*) in the zen manner, meditation involves sitting on a cushion or on a chair and attempting to still both your body and your mind. Movement of any kind, apart from the gentle rise and fall of your breathing, disrupts the flow of meditation. This does not mean that if you are a beginner you must sit like a statue for hours on end. To begin with, five minutes may be quite long enough. But for these five minutes, try as far as is possible to remain still. Almost immediately, you will find that your body wants you to move. Your body is used to controlling you rather than being controlled by you, and it will begin to try and distract you with the urge to shift your position, to scratch your face, to ease some small discomfort or other. Resist these distractions, not by a fierce effort of will but by gently moving your attention away from them. They are there, but they are unimportant.

Consider, too, the movement of your eyes. Whenever we look at an image, we tend to scan it continually from one point of focus to another. If the image is an enigmatic one, we scan it even more, restlessly seeking information to explain it to ourselves. Notice yourself doing this when you begin to meditate with mandalas, and note how difficult it is to keep your eyes still. However, this is not the way to meditate. Take in the whole of the image initially, but having done so allow your eyes to come to rest on one point. Usually, this is the point just above the centre, but there is no fixed rule about this. Do not strain your eyes.

EXPERIENCING STILLNESS

Do not become bored with the mandala. We live in a world of constant, instant gratification. Watch a television programme and notice how quickly each image changes, as if our attention span is so short that we cannot concentrate for more than a few seconds. Meditating on mandalas slows everything down. The frenetic pace of life becomes focused upon a still centre. The mandala is the exact opposite of the flickering, ever-changing television screen.

When you start meditating with mandalas, the novelty of this unusual practice may hold your attention for the first few sessions, but then your restless mind may begin to cast around for new stimuli. Do not allow your mind to distract you. Return to mandala meditation. Remember that this restlessness is simply a result of modern living. The whole purpose of meditation is to free ourselves from this, and to experience the stillness that is our real nature.

Allow them to slip into soft focus if you wish. Blink when you have to, but not more often than necessary. Notice how your eyes, as intent upon movement as your body, try to pull away from this point of focus in order to resume their scanning. Gently resist this attempt.

Almost immediately you will find that thoughts start trying to intrude – thoughts about why you are meditating, about your daily life, about problems with work or with your relationships, about last summer's vacation or about next Christmas. As with bodily distractions, gently move your attention away from these thoughts. You cannot stop them arising, but you can stop them dominating your awareness. Like the body, the mind is used to controlling you, and resents having to relinquish this control during the period of meditation. But you cannot meditate if you are

distracted by thoughts rather than relaxing into stillness.

Similarly, let go of emotions. Anger or resentment at some remembered confrontation with colleagues, fear at the prospect of an impending challenge, sexual desires, happiness at the thought of a new relationship or of some future event, will all, like the body and the mind, try to distract you. Such emotions can emerge without you even realizing it, but they can dominate your mind as much as thoughts. Become aware of them, then let them go.

In order to remain undistracted by your body, by thoughts and by emotions, you need to keep refocusing your attention on the mandala. Vision is one of our strongest senses, and if the vision is held steadily upon an image, this helps to calm the restlessness of body, mind and emotions.

THE ART OF SEEING

We are born with a wish to see meaning in the world, to make sense of experience. It is this wish that leads us as children to ask so many questions of the adults in our lives: "What is this for?" "What does this mean?" "How does this work?" "Why does this happen?" and so on. The search for meaning is further strengthened by our education. We are taught to look for answers, as if everything can be put into words.

However, we are born with a complementary ability to experience things just as they are, without questioning them or finding labels for them. A child can look at a painting and enjoy it for its patterns or colours and no other reason. Unfortunately, as our desire for meaning strengthens, this pure acceptance is educated out of us.

This is one of the reasons why science has become exalted above the arts. Science is serious and purposeful, we are told, while art is at best a pleasurable diversion, and at worst a rather frivolous waste of time.

Thus when we see a picture, even an abstract piece of modern art, we immediately seek its meaning, as if its meaning is something distinct and separate from the picture itself. And when we see a mandala, the same process applies. We want to know what it is trying to say, what it is for. This attempt to learn the secrets of the mandala by questioning it will only distance you from it. Instead, if it doesn't sound too fanciful, look at the mandala in the way that a small child would look at it, attracted by its shape and its colours, but without becoming lost in concepts about it.

As soon as you start meditating with mandalas, your mind will attempt to apply labels to what it is seeing. It will try to tell you the names of the shapes and the colours, to note resemblances between them and other objects, to establish preferences between this shape and that, between that colour and this. Note that this is happening, but do not become distracted by it. The mandala is already teaching you an important lesson. It is demonstrating that we have lost the art of pure seeing. We are so preoccupied with words, labels and concepts that we can no longer see things as they are in themselves. Bring your mind gently back to the pure art of seeing. Try to enter fully into the mandala meditation as a visual experience, no more and no less. The mandala will communicate with you wordlessly. And because pictures and images long predate language in our evolutionary history, it will communicate with you at a deep, primal level of the unconscious mind. The mandala's message has to do with being, not with knowing. Try not to pass judgment upon the mandala, either as something you like or as something you dislike. It just is, in the same way that you just are.

HOW MANDALAS WORK

Like all mandalas, the ones in this book are not artistic constructs, created to look colourful and attractive. Many successful visual artists, like successful poets and musicians, are open to a creative impulse that arises from deep levels of the unconscious. The artist expresses what is given to him or her, not what is put together by conscious thought. ancient Greek sculptors, who produced some of the finest pieces in stone known to humankind, worked on the principle that hidden within the block of stone in front of them was the perfect form. Their task was simply to reveal it. If they allowed their own ideas, their own ego to intrude, then the finished piece was the work of man, not the work of the divine muses who inspired the creative spirit hidden within the stone. In the same way, the modern creative artist has to allow some inner impulse to take over from his or her own mind and express itself *through* the person, rather than *from* the person.

The mandalas in this book capture something of this artistic spirit. They are expressions of the deeper levels of consciousness that are common to us all. Thus when we contemplate them, they help us to access these deeper levels within ourselves. But do not expect too much of the mandalas. They cannot do the work of meditation for us. What they *can* do is provide us with the stimulus, a form of road map which, if we read it well, will guide us toward a level of understanding.

Looking at it like this, mandalas are both static and dynamic. Static in that they represent stillness, but dynamic in that implicit in that stillness there is the concept of movement – both from one feature of the mandala to another, and within the meditator. There is movement from the tensions of the body to a condition of physical relaxation; movement from the turmoil that is the usual state of the mind to the tranquillity that is its real nature; and movement from the habitual distracted and superficial state of consciousness to something much deeper and wiser – movement, in fact, from the circumference of the circle into the heart that is its centre.

We use mandalas by preventing our analytical mind, the mind that governs our waking life, from intruding between us and the visual experience of the mandala. We sit in meditation, with the mandala in front of us, and allow ourselves to take it into our visual space. It as if this visual space, an expression of our consciousness, reaches out to embrace the mandala – or, if you prefer, as if we allow the visual space of the mandala to embrace our consciousness.

BECOMING ONE WITH THE MANDALA

In addition to shapes and colours, some mandalas – particularly those from the Tibetan Buddhist tradition – contain the figures of deities, such as the various Celestial buddhas. These beings are said to be personifications of the various energies that sustain creation, existing both in their own right and as aspects of our own minds. Ultimately, it is said that there is no distinction between these energies and ourselves, for we are all aspects of the unity from which the world of appearances arises.

Traditionally, the meditator seeks to experience the truth of this by incorporating the mandala into his or her own self – this is sometimes referred to as "awakening the mandala within oneself". Becoming one with the mandala in this way is a very advanced practice, undertaken only under the guidance of an experienced meditation teacher. However, even the inexperienced meditator may increasingly feel a sense of strong identification with the mandala, as if it expresses something profound about the self.

Ultimately, there is no distinction between us and the mandala. It is outside ourselves, yet at the same time within the deepest recesses of our minds.

This is why in true meditation, it is important to come to a mandala without preconceptions about its meaning. Like any visual art, the mandala means what it is, not what we can put into words. If the mandala were a language of words, then it would be expressed in writing. Pictures and symbols communicate with a space within ourselves that is far deeper than words, far more basic and primal, and therefore far closer to the creative essence from which all things arise.

WHAT MANDALAS REVEAL

One way of approaching the mandala is as a wise friend who knows us even better than we know ourselves. If we have a wise friend, we do not interrupt him or her, we do not deny what our friend is telling us, we do not come between ourselves and the things that he or she is trying to convey. When you sit in meditation before your mandala, it is important to have the same attitude. The mandala will help you to meditate only if you allow it to do so.

A great Zen master once said to his pupil that the reason the pupil could not make progress was that he had "a too wilful will". The pupil thought that he could not access the life-force within himself unless he "made it happen". The feeling that we must "make it happen" is endemic to our Western mind and modes of thinking. The emphasis is always upon doing it for ourselves, upon learning for ourselves and assessing our own progress. This attitude is a great handicap in the practice of meditation.

Meditation is a process of opening our inner selves and allowing something to express itself that we did not know we possessed. Christianity puts it: "Be still and know that I am God." God, the Kingdom of Heaven, the life-force, the Divine spirit, call it what you will, is already within us. If it were not, we would not exist. Meditation is a process that allows the layer upon layer of conditioning acquired during our lives to be peeled away, so that this creative essence, the real expression of who we are, can reveal itself.

When you are meditating, contemplate the mandala and see what arises. However, if the sensations you are experiencing with a particular mandala disturb you, stop your meditation. The mandala you are working with may not be the right one for you at this time. Perhaps it is taking you too deep, too quickly. Perhaps it is unsuitable for your temperament. On the other hand, adventurous spirits may find that some mandalas are too neutral or too soporific. This is where a good meditation teacher can help: he or she can choose mandalas that are suited to your temperament. If you are working without a teacher, then this is an opportunity to look more closely at yourself. Notice to which mandalas you feel most drawn. Are you someone who seeks gentleness and calm, or an adventurous spirit who likes challenge, confrontation and change? You are who you are. No one temperament is better than another. Never force yourself into a category to which you do not belong. There will always be new mandalas you can use. As you get used to this type of meditation, you may start to see mandalas in the world around you and elements of the world in mandalas.

A MEDITATION ON FORM AND SPACE

The outer world is made up of space as well as form. But we tend to think almost exclusively of the latter, undervaluing the former. Yet the one encloses and defines the other. Artists are often taught to draw the spaces surrounding objects, not the objects themselves. This frees them from preconceptions about how the objects should look. When the drawing is complete, the objects spring to life, as if miraculously, between the drawn spaces.

This meditation is an excellent way of apprehending the realities of space and form, and thus of developing a sense of the unity and interconnectedness of everything that exists. You will need a tea cup or coffee cup for this meditation – something you see every day yet take for granted.

1 Sit cross-legged or in your usual meditation position and focus on your breathing, with eyes closed. When you feel centred, open your eyes and turn your attention from your breathing to the cup in your hand and look at it from all angles. Pay no attention to any thoughts or feelings about the cup that may arise. Ignore what you know of it – its function and its daily usage. Make no judgments. See the cup simply as something occupying space. Take in its contours, colours, angles, texture. See the object as if for the very first time.

2 Now think of the cup as surrounded by empty space, and containing empty space within itself. Which is more important for the cup to function as a cup: the space in and around it or the form of which it is composed? Would it be a cup without either the space or the form?

3 Look around your room. What makes it a room, the walls, or the space they enclose? Which is more important? Look out of the window. Would an object exist as itself if it were not for the space around it?

THE SELF AND SELF-ACCEPTANCE

All meditation is an exercise in self-discovery. For much of the time we assume that we know ourselves, that we know who we are, but in reality much of our mind is unknown territory. We rarely explore the depths of our unconscious, or pause to ask about the meaning and purpose of our existence. We live on the surface of our lives, and in a very real sense are strangers even to ourselves.

The mandala is like a mirror that helps us to discover who we are. If the mandala is a suitable one, it is already a reflection of something deep inside ourselves, a reflection that does not judge or condemn, that does not flatter or deceive, that does not compare us with other people and find us better or worse, that simply reveals to us things as they are. When we stop to think about ourselves we become aware of all sorts of strengths and weaknesses, but the mandala is not interested in these. Like a mirror, it accepts all that it sees. It teaches us not to hide from ourselves. It teaches us to stop pretending that we are somebody we are not and to experience what it is to be ourselves rather than becoming lost in an artificial world of concepts, prejudices and needless hopes and fears about ourselves.

A large part of human suffering arises from our inability to value ourselves. All too often the early, formative years of life have left us with a feeling of inadequacy, no matter how great our achievements. For many of these childhood years people may be more intent on pinpointing our failures and our inadequacies than on drawing attention to our successes. Meditation helps us to let go of some of these misconceptions. It teaches us that we are who we are, and that who we are is the place from which we must start.

Self-acceptance has nothing to do with ego, with developing an inflated view of ourselves, or with hiding from our weaknesses. It has to do with honesty and understanding. You may find that some mandalas in this book prove more helpful as mirrors than others. Feel free to choose between them, but do not reject a mandala simply because it does not seem to work for you initially. The self is a paradox in that it is at one and the same time both very complex and very simple. Like the mandala, it takes time to reveal its secrets.

THE SELF AND ENLIGHTENMENT

The "self" is a rather vague term, but modern psychologists take it to refer both to the picture we have of ourselves – our self-consciousness and our self-image – and the unifying principle that makes us recognizable to ourselves and others as an individual. Buddhism insists that this "self" is subject to constant change, although our memories give us a sense of its continuity through the years.

The various demands made upon us from childhood onward can lead to the self becoming fragmented and subject to inconsistent behaviour and inner conflict. Meditation helps to re-integrate the self and to reveal a deeper aspect of our nature – usually called the "soul" or "spirit" – underlying the impermanent, changing self that we mistakenly believe is who we really are. The recognition of our true nature is sometimes referred to as "enlightenment", and this enlightenment is something that cannot be taught, only directly experienced.

KINDNESS

One of my Tibetan Buddhist meditation teachers used to teach that even if we felt we were able to do little to further our spiritual progress, we could and should always practise kindness. What he meant by this was that kindness is the foundation stone upon which all spiritual progress is built. An act of simple kindness can, in fact, be a perfect action, because it is complete in itself. Opening a window to release a trapped butterfly may seem a small thing to do, yet this is exactly what Christ or the Buddha would do in the same circumstances. The action is exactly what is required by the butterfly in that precise moment of time. Nothing needs to be added to it, and nothing taken from it. By becoming aware of this, and practising kindness in what seem to be the small things of life, we find that it becomes increasingly natural to practise kindness in what we may think of as the big things.

How can meditating on a mandala help to make us kinder people? The answer is simple. A mandala that expresses a deep sense of harmony communicates at an unspoken level the interconnectedness of all things, the value of peace and tranquillity, the natural and spontaneous way in which each element can support and enhance the existence of each of the other elements. Kindness is not an artificial quality grafted upon life, but something intrinsic, that arises of itself once we stop thinking of life as fragmented and individualistic, with each person concerned only for himself or those closest to himself and with no thought for others. The mandala works by virtue of the relationship between each of its parts, which represent not just themselves but an integral aspect of the whole.

As with all mandala practice, avoid keeping thoughts such as these in mind once you enter meditation. If deliberate thought is there, then the process of meditation has already become an artificial exercise, driven by the conscious mind. The mandala must be allowed to speak to the unconscious unprompted, at an entirely intuitive level. Often we become aware of its effect upon us only after the meditation is over, or when we have been working with it for some weeks or months. Harmony, tranquillity and kindness are natural states of the mind, and by allowing the mind to open to the mandala we rediscover these states, and they begin to influence and inform all our actions in both the inner and outer worlds.

LOVE

All the great spiritual traditions of the world teach that love is the essence of all things, that creation arises from and through love and is sustained by love. Those who have had mystical experiences say the same thing. They describe their individual self not only as expanding during the experience into the infinity of pure being, but as feeling the indescribable bliss of this creative, sustaining love. Ever afterwards their lives are changed by this glimpse of ultimate reality. Many of those who are resuscitated from clinical death speak of something similar, and once again the experience can be life-changing.

Love of this kind is very much more than romantic love. It is a unifying, life-enhancing love, which embraces all that is and which subsumes time and space and all that ever was and will be.

Kindness is an expression of love in daily life, but love goes far beyond kindness, in that the experience of it can unify all opposites, reconcile all differences and end all strife and suffering. Mystics tell us that in the experience of this kind of love all mysteries are revealed, including the mysteries of life and death and the mystery of our own being.

This kind of universal love can be experienced through the practice of meditation. As we progress, we usually develop a profound sense of gratitude and acceptance toward the self. In letting go of feelings of dissatisfaction and disappointment, and by ceasing to judge ourselves, we learn self-acceptance. With time, acceptance comes to seem natural, and often it will open out into a love for the self that is felt as gratitude for the gift of existence rather than for the limited and limiting personal ego.

All true mandalas – that is, all mandalas that are created through the intuitive wisdom of the unconscious rather than through the calculating knowledge of the conscious mind – are symbolic representations of love. Thus one does not choose one of these mandalas as specific to love. There is love in them all. At some point, one of the mandalas may appear to "choose" you, in that, with something of the intuition with which it was created, you become aware that it is communicating with you at a particularly deep level. If this is the case, then you may wish to use this mandala more frequently in your meditation than any other. This is perfectly acceptable. The mandalas are not here to be "worked through" in the way in which you would work through exercises in a textbook. They each communicate with you in their

SYMBOLS OF LOVE

Although much used, the heart is in many ways the best symbol for love. Its shape forms an elongated circle. Harmonious and balanced, it resembles also the inverted triangle that is a symbol of the divine life-force streaming down from the heavens into the material world. Another excellent symbol for love is the rose, whose exquisite arrangement of petals forms a beautiful mandala.

Both of these symbols of love can be used in mandala meditation, as can almost any flower and almost any leaf. Scallop shells with their delicate, converging lines are another deeply spiritual mandala. The Earth itself, with its spherical shape, is also a mandala, and a wonderful symbol of love. The Earth sustains us and provides us with food, water and warmth. The sun, which consumes its own being in the process of giving us life, is another perfect mandala and the ultimate symbol of self-sacrificing love.

own way, and after practising with many of them you may find that you have a special relationship with one or other of them, and decide to use that one most often. However, it is worth continuing to work with those that seem to have less to say to you. It may take time for their communications to reveal themselves. Sometimes we learn more about the importance of love through our relationships with difficult people than we do through our friendships. The same can be true of mandalas. Each of those in this book has something to say about love, provided we give it the time and the space in which to say it.

COSMOS

These days, many of us live in towns and cities where light pollution prevents us from seeing the stars and the planets, and so we may rarely give a thought to the vastness of the cosmos in which we live. Even planet Earth seems to be smaller than a speck of dust compared to the vast expanse of this cosmos, and existing on that speck of dust our individual existence hardly seems to merit a mention. However, strange as it may seem, if we go into the desert where we are able to look up at the great bowl of the night sky, the sensation that arises is less one of insignificance than of being an essential part of the sublimity of space. The experience is one of majesty and grandeur, rather than of nothingness. This is because significance has nothing to do with size. The very fact of our existence as part of this vastness is significant in itself, and the mind reaches out spontaneously toward the limitlessness of which it is a part.

Mandalas carry a hint of this cosmic vastness. Some of the traditional Hindu and Tibetan Buddhist mandalas, such as the well-known Sri Yantra, are actually symbolic representations of the unfolding of existence, from the first small point to infinity, which contains everything yet remains empty. Meditating with mandalas can produce timeless moments of mind expansion, in which you seem to transcend the physical body and experience a state of pure consciousness, freed from the constraints of the senses. Recollecting such timeless moments when the meditation is over, there comes a feeling that the mandala has provided a doorway into what is sometimes termed "cosmic consciousness", the realization that you

The Sri Yantra represents cosmic creation. The central point (bindu) symbolizes unity, the divine source. The triangles are the union of Shiva and Shakti, the divine forces of male and female.

are not only an integral and essential part of the cosmos, but that the cosmos is somehow contained within your own mind.

Meditation teachers always warn that one should never strive to achieve this realization. The very act of trying to attain it is a sure way to prevent it from happening. Like everything else of value in meditation, it arises, if it will, of itself. Resist the temptation of trying to see things in the mandala, to make sense of its imagery. And resist the temptation to scan the mandala, eyes flicking from one point to another. Remember that in all mandala meditation it is essential to keep the eyes fixed on one point, usually at or just above the centre of

MEDITATING WITH MYSTERIES

There are far more mysteries in the cosmos than those discovered by astronomers. Space and time themselves, seemingly so familiar to us, are in reality completely unknown quantities. Space is the distance between things, yet what is distance? Time is a process of change, yet what is change? We are located in space, yet space is also located within us, in each atom of our bodies. We are located in time, yet there is no present moment. The more we ponder these questions, the more we realize that space and time, in fact the idea of the cosmos itself, are man-made concepts, formulated in an attempt to explain the inexplicable.

Meditating with a mandala, particularly one from the Hindu or Tibetan Buddhist traditions, can give us a sudden profound insight into the cosmos, an insight that does not solve its mysteries for us, yet perhaps helps us to grasp something of their awesome immensity.

the mandala. And remember too that in meditation you do not have to do things for yourself, to strive for certain effects. All that is needed is that you keep the mind as still as possible, undistracted by thoughts or emotions, or by physical sensations. You did not create the cosmos, and you cannot expect it to reveal itself to you through any efforts of your own.

MAKING YOUR OWN MANDALA

The great Swiss psychiatrist Carl Jung made an extensive study of mandalas, detecting in them a range of potential symbolic meanings. He noticed that as his clients progressed in the course of psychotherapy they spontaneously began to create their own mandalas. For Jung, mandalas were intimately associated with both psychological and spiritual health.

When he built a house for himself at Bollingen, overlooking Lake Geneva, he constructed it in mandala form. You, too, may wish at some stage to make your own mandala.

If you do decide to create a mandala, there are certain guidelines to keep in mind. Firstly, it must not be the result of conscious effort. If you construct a mandala by thinking about it, you will produce something that may look attractive but will essentially be an artificial exercise. The mandala should arise from your unconscious, as if given to you by some power greater than yourself. It may be that your mandala will appear in your mind spontaneously during a meditation session. Or you may wish to sit before a blank sheet of paper, empty your mind of thoughts, and just draw whatever comes to mind. Be patient – it may take several attempts before something arrives that seems to speak directly to you.

Secondly, the mandala is not simply a drawing inside a circle or square. It should have a recognizable symmetry and convey a sense of balance and harmony. It should represent something beyond its immediate appearance, something that you feel will reveal itself little by little as you meditate on it.

Thirdly, never try to force the pace. If something meaningful does not arise, no matter. Don't see this as failure. You may prefer to stay with the mandalas created by others. Traditional mandalas have stood the test of time, meaning that they represent something profound and enduring in ourselves.

Fourthly, don't be afraid to put your mandala to one side if you become dissatisfied with it. Don't allow yourself to become attached to it just because it's your own. It is simply there to help you. It is a tool and and if it ceases to be useful to you, be prepared to let it go.

Instead of creating your own mandala, you may feel moved to adapt one of those in this book. Their purpose is to help you to experiment with meditation and expanding or elaborating one may help you to do so. But once again, be sure to work from your unconscious mind rather than from your normal, analytical consciousness. Don't be tempted to alter a mandala simply to make it look more attractive. Mandalas are things of beauty, but their beauty is an expression of their underlying meaning and harmony. They should never be seen simply as decorative objects. And don't be tempted to try altering one of the mandalas that come from the great spiritual traditions: they already have their own timeless wisdom.

AVOID PRECONCEPTIONS

Only attempt to create your own mandala if you feel drawn to do so. It is not a test of your progress in meditation. If you do wish to create one, work on a sheet of paper of at least A4 size, and equip yourself with several coloured pencils – red, green, yellow and blue as a minimum. Put yourself in a meditative frame of mind. Try to drop any preconceptions of how your mandala should look. Work freehand. You can always carry out minor corrections later if you wish.

Start with a geometrical shape, whichever one comes to mind, then add colours and other shapes as they come to mind. The whole process should be creative and spontaneous, arising from the unconscious rather than from conscious deliberation. Don't try for balance. Draw what comes. The results may surprise you.

Resist the temptation to destroy your mandala if you dislike it. Put it aside, and perhaps try working with it again when the mood takes you.

"The creation of something new is not accomplished by the intellect but by the play instinct acting from inner necessity. The creative mind plays with the objects it loves."
Carl Jung (1875–1961)

CONTINUING THE PRACTICE

It is for you to decide how to continue with mandala meditation. You may wish to include it as part of another meditation programme – for example, one that focuses upon breathing – and use it only from time to time. Alternatively, you may choose to use mandala meditation as your main programme. Either way, to make progress in meditation try to sit each day, either morning or evening or both, for at least 20 to 30 minutes. Build up to this slowly, never trying to force the pace. If possible, try to sit at the same time each day, and establish, if you can, a special place – such as the corner of a room – in which to sit, with a cushion or a chair that you use only for meditation. Wear something light and comfortable, such as a tracksuit or a dressing gown, preferably in a tranquil colour that will harmonize with the tranquillity of your meditation.

If you have created your own mandala, use it if it feels right, but be ready to create a new mandala for yourself if you feel the urge. Notice how the new mandala differs from the old. Meditation is not a form of psychotherapy, such as that used by Carl Jung with his patients, but nevertheless you may be aware of subtle developments in your mandala. Don't try to analyze these too closely, nor consciously to "improve" your mandala. However, note that these differences in shapes and colours may reflect a growing state of inner harmony and balance.

If after persevering with meditation for some time it seems to bring no benefits, don't be discouraged. Changes may have taken place at an unconscious level. And many meditators, although they may stop practising at certain points in their lives, come back to it later. If you find that you have no wish to continue with meditation for the present, put this book to one side, but try not to forget it completely. Like everything to do with meditation, it is here to help you. To adapt the words of one of the greatest of all teachers (Jesus Christ), meditation is made for man and not man for meditation. It remains, like a wise and loyal friend, ever ready to come to our assistance when we need it, such as periods of stress or uncertainty, whenever we need to find the peace that lies always deep within ourselves.

SEEKING THE TRUTH

Dogen, the founder of the Soto Zen tradition, taught that one does not meditate in order to become a buddha, but because meditation is what buddhas do. In other words, the very act of sitting in meditation is the act of a buddha. Dogen is referring, of course, to genuine meditation, not simply to sitting lost in thought. But his teaching makes clear that meditation is not only for advanced practitioners. It belongs to us all, as it is the natural state of the mind when the mind becomes still. Meditation does not add something to the mind that is not already there. It strips away the obscurations that prevent the mind from experiencing its own true nature.

This profound truth is a great incentive to continue practising. In meditation we are re-discovering insights into ourselves that have always been there but are now forgotten – also insights that not only confirm our humanity but reveal that we are spiritual beings, expressions of the unifying creative force from which all things, both seen and unseen, arise.

A CELTIC CROSS

THE CELTIC CROSS COMBINES TWO POWERFUL SYMBOLS: THE CIRCLE,
SUGGESTING INFINITY OR THE ETERNAL; AND THE CROSS, SUGGESTING
THE WORLD OF PHYSICAL FORMS. IN ANCIENT TIMES THE IMAGE
PROBABLY DENOTED CREATIVITY.

1 Look at the two basic forms: in essence, the circle suggests the feminine principle and the cross the masculine principle. The interplay of both is all creation.

2 Now move to a higher level of symbolism, seeing the circle as eternity and the cross as the created world. The arms of the cross represent the points of the compass and the four elements.

3 See the fifth element, spirit, as the circle, which also is the circle of life and the endless path of knowledge, all fused into an all-embracing cosmic harmony. Let this enter your mind like water filling a well.

*"If you want to understand the Creator,
seek to understand created things."*

St Columbanus (c.543–615)

SPIRALS

THE CELTS AND OTHER ANCIENT PEOPLES ARE THOUGHT TO
HAVE USED SPIRALS AS SYMBOLS OF THE SUN, SOURCE OF ALL LIFE.
THIS MANDALA REFLECTS THE UNDYING ENERGY OF THE UNIVERSE —
AS WELL AS THE PROGRESS OF THE SOUL.

1 First, see the spirals of the mandala as the dance of divine solar energy, powering all life and all that exists.

2 Now think of the spirals as your voyage to enlightenment. Progress toward the still centre at the heart of the self, slowly but surely getting closer. The harmony of this mandala evolves out of our essential goodness as we seek and find the truth.

3 In your mind, fuse these meanings together — the cosmic and the personal. Perceive the different spirals as merging into one image that represents the growth of nature and the growth of the soul, the flow of the cosmos and the flow of your own understanding, the creation and dissolution of the world and your own self within the world.

"The Sun, hearth of affection and of life,
pours ardent love on the delighted Earth."

Arthur Rimbaud (1854–1891)

THUNDERBIRD

FOR NATIVE AMERICANS THE GREAT SPIRIT MANIFESTED
HIMSELF IN VARIOUS NATURAL FORMS, INCLUDING THUNDERBIRD,
GUARDIAN OF THE SKY, WHO WAS ENGAGED IN ENDLESS BATTLE
WITH THE SERPENTS OF THE UNDERWORLD.

1 Look at the bird in the centre of this mandala: Thunderbird. This can be seen as symbolizing the source of active good in the world, the energy that nourishes our virtues and keeps us alert to all moral dangers.

2 Now contemplate the spiral pattern that surrounds Thunderbird – representing the endless flowering of creation within the transparency of pure mind.

3 Take the bird's energies into your mind as a totem of your spiritual self-knowledge. Whatever your beliefs, this powerful image of the natural world, a bird at home in the storm, can help you to affirm your purpose.

"Listen to the voice of nature, for it holds treasures for us all."

Huron saying

A TRISKELE

IN ITS THREE LINKED SPIRALS, THE TRISKELE IS TYPICALLY CELTIC.
IT DENOTES THE SUN, THE AFTERLIFE AND REINCARNATION.
THIS MANDALA MEDITATION MAY ALSO GENERATE BENEFICIAL
ENERGIES IF YOU ARE PREGNANT.

1 Trace in your mind the continuous line of the triple spiral. This, like the endless knot (see page 139), suggests the endless repetition of life's cycles – a life-force restlessly manifesting itself, and the eternity that is implied by such a perspective.

2 Now see this life-force framed within the context of eternal spirit – as reflected in the perfect outer circle of the mandala.

3 Take into your mind this perfect balance of being and becoming, of eternal emptiness and vibrant creation, and let these harmonies radiate through your mind, into your body, heart and bloodstream. You are endlessly creative, even as you abide in the stillness of the spirit.

"Every creation originates in love."

Lu Xun (1881–1936)

A HEXAGRAM

THE HEXAGRAM IS A PAIR OF INTERLOCKING TRIANGLES,
REPRESENTING UNITY IN DUALITY. IN JUDAISM THE SYMBOL IS KNOWN
AS THE STAR OF DAVID, AND IS ALSO ASSOCIATED WITH SOLOMON.
HEXAGRAMS ALSO APPEAR IN HINDU MANDALAS.

1 Identify the upward-pointing triangle, which is masculine and symbolizes fire; and the downward-pointing one, which is feminine and denotes water.

2 Observe the upper half of the upward triangle, with the base of the downward triangle crossing through it: this is the symbol for air. Then observe the lower half of the downward triangle, again with a horizontal bar across it: this is the symbol for earth. The mandala, then, contains all four elements.

3 Take the mandala as a whole into your mind. As you do so, you are absorbing all the elements, all creation. The fifth element, spirit, denoted by the outer circle, is the medium through which your inner life unfolds.

*"Those who worship Me with devotion,
they are in Me and I am in them."*

The Bhagavad Gita (*c.*5th century BC)

THE PILGRIM'S MAZE

THE LABYRINTH WAS ONCE A SYMBOL OF MORAL CONFUSION,
BUT IN THE MIDDLE AGES CHRISTIANS BEGAN TO SEE IT AS
THE TRUE WAY OF BELIEF. THIS MANDALA IS BASED ON THE MAZE
ON THE FLOOR OF CHARTRES CATHEDRAL, FRANCE.

1 Follow the labyrinth from its entrance (at the bottom) all the way to the floral device at its centre. You should not lose your way, because the labyrinth is unicursal − that is, it has no junctions. But if you forget where you are, go back to the start and try again.

2 As you get closer to the centre, imagine travelling deeper and deeper into the self. The labyrinth is your physical incarnation, the life you lead on Earth; and, at the same time, it is the challenges that you face in following your spiritual destiny.

3 Once you reach the centre, view it as a tunnel that leads down into the page. Step into this tunnel. For many the labyrinth continues, but for you the path is now straight − as long as you keep the purity of heart that your pilgrimage has brought you.

"The perfect way is only difficult for those who pick and choose."

Seng-ts'an (c.520–606)

PERFECT SYMMETRY

THIS MANDALA, LIKE THE SRI YANTRA (SEE PAGE 36), CAN HELP
THE MEDITATOR TO GO BACK SYMBOLICALLY TO THE MOMENT OF
CREATION. IT REMINDS US THAT THERE IS NO FUNDAMENTAL
DIFFERENCE BETWEEN SUBJECT AND OBJECT.

1 Appreciate the different shapes of the mandala, starting with the triangular segments, denoting the physical world, and turning next to the concentric circles, suggesting all-embracing spiritual perfection. Note also the "tear splashes" around the edges – suggestive of joy and sorrow.

2 Look at the criss-crossing lines, going off in different directions.

These represent the male and female principles that give rise, in their interplay, to creation. The central cluster of circles is the divine source of all life, pulsing with energy, as if the sun had been squeezed to the size of a button.

3 Let all the energies of the mandala float deeper and deeper into your consciousness, until your mind achieves a perfect and peaceful resonance.

*"Everything in the universe is within you.
Ask for everything from yourself."*

Jalil al–Din Rumi (1207–1273)

THE WHEEL OF TRUTH

THE WHEEL IN THIS MANDALA, BASED ON A TIBETAN ORIGINAL,
SYMBOLIZES THE TEACHINGS OF BUDDHISM, INCLUDING THE GOALS
OF ABSOLUTE SELFLESSNESS AND TRUE PERCEPTION. ITS CENTRAL
SPIRALS DENOTE WISDOM AND COMPASSION.

1 Look at the square frame in which the mandala sits – representing the solidity and density of the material world.

2 Now turn to the wheel itself. The hub is a double yin-yang symbol, around which are circles showing the steps toward enlightenment. The wheel's eight spokes symbolize the Buddha's Eightfold Path: right speech, right action, right livelihood, right effort, right mindfulness, right concentration, right view and right thought.

3 Look at the stylized lotus designs on the rim of the wheel, reflecting the pure heart that is filled with love and wisdom. Absorb the wheel into yourself as a guide and commitment to purity and wholeness.

"Happiness is when what you think, what you say and what you do are in harmony ..."

Mahatma Gandhi (1869–1948)

A BIRD'S NEST

MANDALAS BASED WHOLLY ON THE NATURAL WORLD
HAVE A UNIVERSAL DIMENSION, FREE OF SPECIFIC CULTURAL
SYMBOLISM. HERE, THE STARTING POINT IS THE ORIGIN OF LIFE
EXPRESSED IN A COMMONPLACE FORM — THE EGG

1 Look at the elements of the mandala and imagine yourself looking down onto the scene – a bird's nest with three eggs in it right in the centre of a tree's leafy canopy, with four other, surrounding nests lower down the tree.

2 Concentrate on the three eggs, first as pure shape and colour. Then lose yourself in the intricate pattern of twigs in the nest.

3 Now begin to imagine the scene as a real, three-dimensional situation. Imagine how high you are above the ground in which the tree is rooted. Imagine the sounds of birdsong all around.

4 Lastly, concentrate on the individual lives cocooned in these three eggs – the wonder of genetic inheritance, the miracle of nature's ingenuity.

"As adults we may again experience birth, the cracking open of a shell, the attainment of a radical new vision."

Eduardo Cuadra (1820–1903)

A WATERFALL

THIS MANDALA SHOWS LIFE AS A POOL IN THE ENDLESS FLOW
OF TIME. THERE ARE DANGERS (THE CROCODILES) BUT IF WE ARE
PURE WE WILL COME TO NO HARM. BY ACCEPTING THAT WE ARE
PART OF NATURE, WE GAIN SELF-UNDERSTANDING.

1 Start by looking at the source of the waters, high in the mountains. The rainbow is like a halo, symbolizing the beauty and sacredness of life when sunlight (the divine) shines through water droplets (our bodies) in the atmosphere.

2 Now think of yourself as the swimmer, free and naked in the pool. You immerse yourself fully in nature, in the way things are. You rejoice in your being, in your incarnation within a lifetime.

3 You understand that any physical dangers are an integral part of nature, too – which is why the crocodiles in the mandala appear to flow like streams themselves. Accept that the rainbow blesses the crocodiles as well as the swimmer. Life is a constantly changing balance of forces.

"Bodies come and go like clothes."

Sri Sankara (*c.*788–*c.*820)

FIRE AROUND THE LOTUS

HERE THE DEEPLY SPIRITUAL LOTUS IS SURROUNDED BY A RING
OF FIRE, SUGGESTING PURIFICATION. THIS MANDALA ALSO SHOWS
A FOUR-GATED PALACE, DENOTING SHELTER OR SAFETY,
UNIVERSAL ORDER AND THE BALANCE OF OPPOSITES.

1 Start by contemplating the outer
ring of fire – a complex symbol with
overtones of purification through
destruction, the light of wisdom and
regeneration. You are not afraid to burn
off your attachments.

2 Now look at the lotus, which flowers
within your mind as your spiritual
vision becomes focused.

3 Lastly, take your mind into the
four-gated palace at the heart of
the mandala. Awakened as you are,
you find the emptiness of the palace
immeasurably rich and nourishing. You
are at peace.

"Words are only painted fire; a look is the fire itself."

Mark Twain (1835–1910)

THE GREEN MAN

AN ANCIENT PAGAN SYMBOL, THE GREEN MAN IS ALSO FOUND
CARVED ON MEDIEVAL CHURCHES, A REMNANT OF MORE
PRIMAL BELIEFS. HE SYMBOLIZES THE CYCLE OF LIFE, DEATH AND
REBIRTH, AND THE GREEN SAP OF THE LIFE–FORCE.

1 Look at the face camouflaged among the greenery of foliage. Now look closer and notice that leaves are coming out of the man's mouth and flesh – he is an incarnation of nature, not merely an onlooker.

2 Recognize that in many ways we too are incarnations of nature and, conversely, that nature participates in the spirit, in the sense that natural beauty could not exist were it not for our own perception of divine harmony even in the wilderness or wild wood, far from humankind.

3 Take the mandala into your mind as an image of the unity of the cosmos and of our kinship with animals, trees and flowers.

"Shall I not have intelligence with the earth?
Am I not partly leaves and vegetable mould myself?"

Henry David Thoreau (1817–1862)

An Octopus

THE OCTOPUS IS A SYMBOL OF THE UNFOLDING OF CREATION
FROM ITS MYSTIC CENTRE, AS WELL AS AN EXAMPLE OF OTHERNESS.
THIS MANDALA COMBINES THESE MEANINGS TO GIVE US A
SENSE OF WHO WE ARE AND WHAT LIFE IS.

1 Look at the random spirals of the octopus's eight arms. They suggest the endless energies of life as it unfolds out of the mystic centre of creation.

2 Now think of the octopus as a creature with its own brain and its own individual mental landscape – not a mind as such, but a kind of world-view nonetheless.

3 The octopus squirts a cloud of black ink around itself to confuse its enemies. But you are not its enemy. You co-exist with the octopus and wish it no harm. Indeed, you respect its vital essence and the validity of the life it leads. Its strange beauty is a precious aspect of your cosmos.

*"The enlightened soul is open to wonder.
Every marvel of nature mirrors the miracle of being alive."*

Modern meditation from Lisbon

FLOATING LOTUS

THE BEAUTY OF THE LOTUS IS THAT IT REMAINS UNTOUCHED
BY EITHER THE WATER OR THE MUD THAT NOURISH IT —
SUGGESTING OUR UNDEFILED SPIRIT. THIS MANDALA HAS
AN OVERHEAD VIEWPOINT, LIKE AN AERIAL PHOTOGRAPH.

1 Look at the swirling waters of the created world – they have their own divine beauty, and so are enclosed within a flower-shaped pool surround.

2 Turn your gaze to the central, circular pool of water. As if by magic, it reflects the starry night above. This is an image of the awesome vastness of the cosmos.

3 Contemplate the lotus at the heart of the mandala, with its central yin-yang symbol. The lotus denotes pure spirit, embracing the complementary opposites that exist in this world and the cosmos.

4 Lastly, let these various beauties – water, sky, stars, flower, and our own contradictory natures – harmonize in your mind and bring you peace.

"Those who know the truth are not equal to those who love the truth."

Confucius (551–479 BC)

HEART LOTUS

THIS IS THE MIDDLE CHAKRA IN OUR SYSTEM OF CHAKRAS
(ENERGY POINTS) WITHIN THE BODY. THE LOTUS SUGGESTS
SPIRITUALITY, WHICH WE CAN FIND IN OUR HEARTS.
THE CENTRAL HEXAGRAM ENCLOSES THE "SEED" SOUND, "YAM".

1 Look at the circle that frames the mandala – it is an image of spiritual perfection.

2 Then contemplate the leaves and petals of the lotus, which continue this symbolism. The lotus can flower within ourselves and enable us to transcend suffering. As we flower spiritually, our hearts spill out love and compassion – tender as the lotus petals, strong as the life-force itself.

3 Lastly, gaze at the central hexagram, with its intersecting triangles, representing the dualities of our existence. To open the pure heart fully we must bring into balance the complementary aspects of our life – male and female, light and shadow, mind and body, practicality and spirituality.

*"Heart is called the place where there is a repose
in the pure light and pure consciousness."*

Abhinavagupta (c.975–c.1025)

SUN LOTUS

THE CENTRE OF THIS MANDALA IS A SOLAR SPIRAL FROM WHICH
THE SUN'S RAYS RADIATE. THIS IS PLACED WITHIN A LOTUS,
WHICH DEPICTS BEAUTY GROWING FROM MUD, JUST AS THE SOUL
RISES FROM CONFUSION TO ENLIGHTENMENT.

1 Look at the outside of the mandala, the circle, which suggests perfection. Then contemplate the lotus flower, a symbol of potential perfection, within that frame.

2 Now turn your attention to the heart of the mandala. The spiral here could represent the meditator's journey into the self – as well as the primal flow of energy that makes the world what it is.

3 Feel how you relate to these different elements: the perfection (outer circle) that you can find within yourself if your heart is pure; the flowering of spirituality from the soil of incarnation (lotus); the energy of the sun (spiral), which drives your Earthly being.

4 Let these elements fuse together in your mind, as in the totality of the mandala. Find peaceful self-awareness in this thought.

"Without self-knowledge we are sundials in the shade."

Modern meditation from Rome

Nature's Harmony

CONCENTRIC CIRCLES BRING A SPIRITUAL PURITY TO THIS MANDALA,
BASED ON THE ORDER OF THE COSMOS WITH ITS BEAUTIFUL LIFE
AND EARTH FORMS. THE LOTUS DESIGN ON THE OUTER CIRCLE EMPHASIZES
THE SPIRITUAL DIMENSION.

1 Look at the sky, with its heavenly bodies, in the corners of this mandala. Then progress through the outer frame of lotus motifs. You find yourself symbolically in the realm of the mountains and the clouds.

2 Pass through the next circle into the greenery of nature, where trees, plants, birds and insects abound. This is Eden, the natural paradise.

3 Finally, penetrate to the mystic centre, which borrows from nature to express its divine creativity. Imagine the central circle as the cross-section of a shaft of light that drills into your deepest self to awaken the spirit.

*"All things share the same breath — the beast, the tree, the man.
The air shares its spirit with all the life it supports."*

Chief Seattle (1786–1866)

CRANES AMONG CLOUDS

IN THE JAPANESE TRADITION CRANES ARE SYMBOLS OF
GOOD FORTUNE. CLOUDS SUGGEST THE CHANCE EVENTS THAT
TEMPORARILY CAST SHADOWS OVER OUR LIVES. THIS MEDITATION
COMBINES THESE EVOCATIVE SYMBOLS

1 Identify the main elements of the mandala – the cranes, the blue sky, the clouds that sometimes block flying cranes from our view.

2 Keeping the mandala in your field of vision, let the details dissolve in your mind and give way to a view of empty blue sky. Let this blank sky fill your mind.

3 Visualize clouds forming a random pattern across this sky. They float across your consciousness. Then visualize a loose flock of cranes flying across the vista, passing in and out of the clouds randomly. Each crane that appears brings blessings into your life. Some of the cranes fly right through the clouds – like a happy outcome emerging from risk. Give thanks for such good fortune.

"Fortune will call at the smiling gate."

Japanese proverb

THE FLUTE PLAYER

THE FLUTE PLAYER IS AN IMAGE USED BY THE 13TH-CENTURY
PERSIAN POET RUMI TO SYMBOLIZE OUR LONGING FOR UNION WITH
THE SPIRIT. THE FLUTE YEARNS TO JOIN ITS SOURCE — THE REEDBED
FROM WHICH IT WAS ORIGINALLY CUT.

1 Look at the flute player playing at sunset. Behind him are the clumps of reeds from which the flute was cut. Imagine that the music, the flute and the player are all one, and all feeling the call of the divine.

2 Think of the flute player's music as a soundless expression of his unconscious mind – a flowering of the soul in its purity.

3 Look at the other forms of life in the mandala – the waterlilies and fishes. Think of these too as yearning for unity: all the cosmos is one.

*"Pure soul, how long will you travel? You are the King's falcon.
Fly back toward the Emperor's whistle!"*

Jalil al–Din Rumi (1207–1273)

YIN-YANG

THE TAI CHI, OR YIN-YANG, SYMBOL AT THE CENTRE OF
THIS MANDALA IS AN ANCIENT EASTERN IMAGE REPRESENTING
THE BALANCE BETWEEN OPPOSING AND COMPLEMENTARY FORCES
THAT CONSTITUTE OUR WORLD.

1 Look at the flowers and other motifs, and appreciate the contrast of the squares (the material world) with the circles (eternity).

2 Now look at the central yin-yang image. See how each of the two elements contains the seed of its opposite. Relate this to the opposites balanced within you: masculine/feminine, action/stillness, insight/compassion, outward/inward, and so on.

3 Look at the smaller yin-yang symbols and notice their position, between the square and the surrounding circle, touching both. Think of them as atoms that occur in everything, the universal stuff of existence.

4 See the mandala with all its embellishments as both the cosmos and the individual cell – like life itself.

"Clay is fired to make a pot.
The pot's use comes from its emptiness."

Tao Te Ching (6th century BC)

THE FLOWER OF SELF

THIS IS A MANDALA IN WHICH TO LOSE AND FIND ONESELF.
IT REFLECTS FLOWERING SELF-AWARENESS, THE ETERNAL SELF IN
FULL BLOOM, THE UNCHANGING ESSENCE AT THE CORE OF ALL
OUR REPEATED DAYS, MONTHS AND YEARS.

1 Visually, trace the green, wave-like shoots that surround the central flower. They are lines of energy, each a wave of becoming, revealing a flower of being. The bees are in perpetual motion, their wings beating faster than the eye can see.

2 Now turn your attention to the central flower. Take its many-petalled radiance into your mind, where it rests as a still reflection of your many-petalled self, the flowering of being beyond becoming.

3 There are two bees on the petals of this flower, but you do not brush them away: you are happy to let them live their fleeting moments on the wonderful flower of the spirit – like our own lifetimes.

"Truth is inside you. To see it you must open the inner eye."
The Buddha (c.563–c.483 BC)

THE STAR IN THE WELL

LOOKING DEEP INTO OUR SELVES WE SEE OUR GREATEST RICHES —
SUGGESTED BY A STAR IN A WELL. LIKE ANY STAR, IT IS
UNTOUCHABLE BUT REAL. IT GIVES US EVERYTHING
AND NOTHING. IT IS THE OBJECT OF ALL OUR QUESTING.

1 Identify the different stages and planes of the mandala: the outer world of nature, the surround of paving, the square base within that, and lastly the hollow drop of the well itself.

2 Contemplate the star that you can see reflected in the water of the well. It shines brightly despite the darkness and the distance.

3 Think of yourself as looking right into the innermost depths of your own spirit. The deeper you penetrate, the brighter you shine. Your star is unique and beautiful, and can never be extinguished.

"As far as we can discern, the sole purpose of human existence is to kindle a light in the darkness of mere being."

Julian of Norwich (1342–*c*.1416)

THE SALMON OF KNOWLEDGE

BECAUSE OF ITS AMAZING ABILITY TO CROSS OCEANS AND FIND
ITS WAY UNERRINGLY TO ITS SPAWNING GROUNDS, THE CELTS
ASSOCIATED THE SALMON WITH PROPHECY. MEDITATE ON THE
SALMON TO COME CLOSER TO YOUR INTUITIVE WISDOM.

1 You are in the branches of a tree looking down. Two salmon are swimming in a circular pool below you. You can see also the leaves of the surrounding trees and the pool's decorative surround. Little hazelnuts are floating on the water's surface: these too are symbolic of prophetic insight.

2 Think of the salmon as a living yin-yang symbol: one is male, the other female. Acknowledge both the male and female sides within yourself, as together they give you the gift of insight.

3 Draw the whole image within yourself. Feel the depths of your intuition. All reason can do is count the fish and the hazelnuts and decorate the pool edge; intuition can penetrate the inner depths, where love and truth are to be found.

*"Let your hook be always cast. In the pool
where you least expect it, there will be fish."*

Ovid (43 BC–AD 17)

JEWELS

GEMS WERE OBJECTS OF WONDER TO THE ANCIENTS, DIVINE
FORCES CONJURING LIGHT FROM DARK EARTH. IN EASTERN THOUGHT,
JEWELS SIGNIFIED SPIRITUAL ILLUMINATION. THIS BEJEWELLED
MANDALA CONTAINS THE YIN-YANG SYMBOL, TOO.

1 Look at the different jewels and their colours. There are diamonds, denoting radiance and integrity; rubies, denoting love and courage; pearls, denoting intuition and feminine wisdom; sapphires, denoting peace and harmony.

2 See the pattern of the jewels in their delicate settings as being symbolic of the radiant and intricate order of the universe, illuminated by the intensely beautiful light of the spirit.

3 Let your eyes rest on the yin-yang symbol – the creative interplay of opposites at the heart of our existence. The spirit adorns and transcends the body, as the jewels adorn and transcend male and female, light and dark, action and feeling.

"Knowing what is enough is wealth."

Tao Te Ching (6th century BC)

LOVING KINDNESS

THIS TIBET-INSPIRED MANDALA ENABLES YOU TO
SUFFUSE YOUR WHOLE MIND WITH POSITIVE FEELINGS
TOWARD OTHERS — NOT ONLY LOVED ONES AND FRIENDS,
BUT ALSO ACQUAINTANCES AND EVEN STRANGERS.

1 Imagine a loved one sitting in the mandala's centre, where the seated figure is. Dwell on the qualities you admire so much in this person. Visualize him or her bathed in your love.

2 Contemplate the four symbols within the T shapes: dove (peace), hands (warmth), fire (purity) and eye (empathy). Identify all these ingredients in the quality of your love.

3 Visualize family and friends in particular niches inside the mandala. Beyond the central square are mere acquaintances and beyond the outer circle a number of strangers.

4 Welling up around the central figure and endlessly spilling outward, feel your love pouring out of you and energizing everyone. The strangers receive the same quality of love as your loved one — a love that is undiminished by distance.

*"Meditate on love so that you long for
the welfare of all, even your enemies."*

The Buddha (c.563–c.483 BC)

DOLPHINS AT PLAY

THE DOLPHIN IS PLAYFUL AND COMMUNICATIVE.
INSTINCTIVELY IT TAKES JOY IN EACH MOMENT. DOLPHIN
SYMBOLISM IS COMBINED HERE WITH IMAGERY OF THE OCEAN,
FROM WHICH ALL LIFE EVOLVED.

1 Look at the dolphins swimming in the centre and the two dolphins performing acrobatics around them. Their ability to break free of their own element, the water, and dance in another, the air, suggests our own potential for liberation once we have embraced the power of the spirit.

2 Contemplate the circle that the two dophins make in their dance of joy. The circle suggests both spiritual perfection and the endless cycle of life, rising and falling, coming and going, like the dolphins.

3 Think of the vastness of the ocean, and the infinite expanse of sky above it. Taking the mandala into your mind, absorb the harmony of the cosmos. Our lives are gleaming droplets of water within the shining ocean of being.

"Grace is a gravity that has learnt how to play."

Modern meditation from Los Angeles

A WATER GARDEN

A GARDEN IS THE UNIVERSAL SYMBOL OF
HARMONY IN NATURE AND OF THE HUMAN SOUL
WHICH, JUST LIKE A GARDEN, MUST BE IN HARMONY
WITH ITSELF IN ORDER TO FIND PEACE.

1 The life-giving powers of the water, which plays endlessly through the fountain, give sustenance to the fish, just as love gives sustenance to the soul.

2 The paving around the pond is made up of uneven blocks, perfectly fitted together – a symbol of the work done by unconditional love and of love's tolerance of imperfections.

3 Notice that you cannot focus on all four of the trees that flourish outside of the garden at once, but that you can hold them at the edge of awareness, just as love can contain all things. Think of love as the soil, rain and roots of existence.

"You are an ocean of knowledge hidden in a dew drop."

Jalil al–Din Rumi (1207–1273)

JACOB'S LADDER

IN GENESIS, JACOB DREAMS OF ANGELS ASCENDING AND
DESCENDING A LADDER BETWEEN HEAVEN AND EARTH.
EVEN IN OUR PHYSICAL EXISTENCE WE CAN ENJOY INTIMATIONS
OF THE DIVINE — AS LONG AS WE ARE OPEN TO LOVE.

1 Start by gazing at the Earthly city. Its inhabitants are caught up in their various preoccupations. Few of the inhabitants even notice the ladder to Heaven: it exists on a different scale from the mundane.

2 Now look at Heaven. Its gates are within you, just as the mandala itself will be within you as soon as you absorb the whole image into your mind.

3 Look at the angels moving back and forth between Heaven and Earth. Their love for the divine, and the love shown by the divine to them, keeps them airborne. Think of them as messengers showing you the way.

4 Lastly, review the journey ahead, up the ladder and into the spiritual world. The angels will help you. Love provides the energy.

*"Be not forgetful to entertain strangers, for thereby
some have entertained angels unawares."*

Hebrews 13:2

TRANSFORMATIONS

BUTTERFLIES DENOTE TRANSFORMATION — OUR AWAKENING
FROM THE DOMINANCE OF THE EGO TO A MATURE SELF-AWARENESS.
LOVE ENABLES US TO TURN OUR ENERGIES BOTH INWARD
(TO TRUTH) AND OUTWARD (TO COMPASSION).

1 Look at the butterflies in the image and choose one at random. Mentally trace its life-cycle back through the different phases: butterfly back to chrysalis, chrysalis back to caterpillar, caterpillar back to egg.

2 Now focus on the caterpillar in the centre of the mandala. Think of the potential for radical change inherent in the creature.

3 Now think of this potential for transformation in the very part of yourself that absorbs the image of the mandala. Sense your capacity for giving and receiving love in abundance, and relish the blessings that such love will bring you.

"All things are complete within ourselves."

Mencius (*c.*390–*c.*305 BC)

A Dove of Peace

THE DOVE IS THE MOST SPIRITUAL OF BIRD SYMBOLS.
IN ADDITION TO ITS UNIVERSAL IMPORTANCE AS AN EXPRESSION
OF PEACE AND RECONCILIATION, IT CONJURES UP THE PURIFIED
SOUL — OR, IN CHRISTIAN TERMS, THE HOLY SPIRIT.

1 Within the outer circle of the mandala, which indicates perfection, contemplate the endless yet restless pattern as an image of Earthly energies. Within this is a rainbow pattern, a beautiful manifestation of the life-giving spirit of the sun.

2 Now focus on the dove with its olive branch, a symbol of salvation. The dove has materialized out of pure spirit – like your own most profound qualities of love and peace. Hold the bird in your gaze as if you are seeing it through a telescope. Its background is eternity.

3 Take this dove into your mind, and relax in the knowledge that it is completely at home there. You have recognized its sign and welcome the bird and its message of peace.

"Peace brings love as love brings peace. The perfect form is the circle."

Modern meditation from Sydney,

AVALOKITESHVARA

THIS IS THE NAME GIVEN IN TANTRIC BUDDHISM TO THE
BODHISATTVA (ENLIGHTENED BEING) OF COMPASSION.
HE RADIATES SELF-SACRIFICING LOVE — DENYING HIMSELF
ENTRY TO NIRVANA UNTIL ALL OTHERS CAN ENTER AS WELL.

1 Any depiction of Avalokiteshvara compels our gaze and demands our profound admiration. Feel the energy of his goodness. It is this that enables us to accept a one-dimensional painting as a deeply benevolent presence.

2 The bodhisattva sits in the lotus position on a lotus flower. Contemplate the perfection he has chosen as his setting.

3 Two of Avalokiteshvara's hands express devotion, while the other two hold a rosary and a lotus. The rosary enables him to count the repetitions of his mantra, "Om Mani Padme Hum", which liberates all beings from suffering. He is weightless, like an image in a mirror. He transcends all concepts — including the idea that he exists only in another dimension. Meditate and you will find him inside yourself.

"No act of kindness, however small, is ever wasted."

Aesop (620–560 BC)

THE DREAM FLAG

A TIBETAN MEDITATION MASTER ONCE SAW A DOUBLE-SCROLLED
FLAG IN A DREAM. HE PREDICTED THAT WHEREVER THIS
BANNER FLEW, THE BUDDHA'S COMPASSION WOULD SPREAD.
THIS FLAG MAKES AN ENLIGHTENING MANDALA.

1 Look at the colours of the flag at the centre of this mandala. Understand the blue as Heaven, denoting spiritual insight, and the yellow as earth, meaning our physical world. Observe how the blue and yellow, spirit and body, are dependent on each other.

2 Now think of the blue as wisdom and the yellow as compassion – two complementary aspects of spiritual self-fulfilment. Again, the interlocking design suggests how inseparable these qualities are.

3 Visualize the dream flag unifying wisdom and compassion as it undulates in the wind.

"What we have to learn to do, we learn by doing."

Aristotle (384–322 BC)

THE ROSE OF PURE LOVE

THIS MANDALA IS THE ROSE CROSS, A SYMBOL THAT GAVE
ITS NAME TO THE MYSTIC ORDER OF THE ROSICRUCIANS.
THE CROSS IMPLIES THE FOUR CARDINAL DIRECTIONS, WHILE
THE ROSE SUGGESTS PURE LOVE. BOTH SYMBOLIZE SACRIFICE.

1 Consider the cross, which incarnates the spirit in the physical world. So powerful a symbol is the cross that we can readily imagine its central point behind the rose. It gives support to the rose, whose flowering transcends it.

2 Look at all the petals of the rose, beautifying the world. Think of them as the unfolding of love within your own heart.

3 Take the mandala into your inner self, where the rose manifests selfless love, compassion and spiritual awareness.

"The heart's message cannot be delivered in words."

Mu-mon Gensen (1322–1390)

ISLANDS

NONE OF US IS AN ISLAND: WE ARE ALL JOINED TO EACH
OTHER BY BRIDGES OF THE SPIRIT. THIS MANDALA TRANSLATES
THIS UNIVERSAL METAPHOR INTO A REPRESENTATION OF
THE JOURNEY FROM THE SELF TO OTHER PEOPLE.

1 The starting point is the Earthly city. Think of its millions of individuals, all with their unique lives and circumstances, dreams and worries. All are strangers to you.

2 Now think of an archipelago of desert islands. Each has people stranded on it, refugees from the overcrowded city. They stand at different ends of their islands, unable to connect with each other.

3 In your mind, set out on a voyage to each island in turn to bring its inhabitants together in neighbourly love through the power of your own love for all humankind.

4 Finally, take the whole mandala into your heart. See the islanders smiling at each other rather than looking out to sea.

"The only way to have a friend is to be one."

Ralph Waldo Emerson (1803–1882)

A SNOWFLAKE

THE SNOWFLAKE IS FLEETINGLY BEAUTIFUL: WE SCARCELY
HAVE TIME TO ADMIRE IT BEFORE IT MELTS. SUCH IS THE WAY
OF THE WORLD: OUR LIVES, OUR LOVES, ARE ENDLESS CHANGE.
BUT AT THE CENTRE IS THE UNCHANGING SPIRIT.

1 Look at the snowflake in this mandala, one of an infinite number of snowflakes, yet complete and perfect within itself. Observe its perfect symmetry, and be aware as you appreciate the design that no other snowflake in the entire cosmos is identical to this one. Let this thought sink into your mind. Spend a few minutes relishing this frequent miracle.

2 Consider the snowflake's intrinsic strength, which comes from its unique beauty. The snowflake is fleeting yet flawless.

3 Imagine that the snowflake is on the point of melting. You are observing it in the moment of its being, from the fleeting viewpoint of your own lifetime.

"Weak overcomes strong, soft overcomes hard."

Tao Te Ching (6th century BC)

Sailing the Storm

STORMY SEAS HAVE TESTED THE FORTITUDE OF MANY A SAILOR.
THIS MANDALA SHOWS A SHIP IN PERIL. USE IT TO FIND
YOUR OWN RESERVES OF COURAGE, AND AS A SPIRITUAL
COMPASS WITH WHICH TO PLOT A SAFE COURSE.

1 You are looking down on a sailing ship from a bird's-eye view. You are safe, dry and calm, but the ship is in trouble – buffeted by gigantic waves, sails threatened by lightning, torrential rain lashing down on the crew.

2 Now scan the mandala as a whole, and notice its harmony. Appreciate that a world where ships can be lost to violent storms is still a beautiful world, and that even in extreme danger you have the resources of spirit to give you strength.

3 Look at the four compasses in the mandala – your tools to steer by. Perhaps these are love, faith, acceptance and compassion.

4 Now look again at the mandala as a whole. See it as reflecting life's totality, with all its challenges and contradictions.

"Only that which cannot be lost in a shipwreck is yours."

Al-Ghazzali (1058–1111)

A SAMURAI SWORD

THE SWORD IS A SYMBOL OF AUTHORITY AND DECISIVENESS.
THIS MANDALA SHOWS A SWORD GUARD SURROUNDED BY FOUR
SWORDS AND THEIR SCABBARDS. MEDITATE ON IT WHEN PREPARING
FOR A LIFE CHANGE OR A BOLD DECISION.

1 Look at the central circle, and within that the decorative cross – an image of creation within spiritual perfection.

2 Now look at the swords and scabbards. They indicate the decision itself. Use them, if you wish, to check that your resolve is firm. To do this, think of the four pairs of swords and scabbards as a progressive scale, ranging through possibly, probably, certainly,

inevitably. Can you move through this scale without hestitation?

3 Lastly, make your decision to act in the way that you believe is right. Focus your will on moving through the centre of the mandala. The flowing embellishments around the centre suggest right action, in accordance with natural law.

"Confusions and dangers are nothing but the mind."

Dogen (1200–1253)

ETERNAL FEMININE

THIS MANDALA ENCLOSES FEMININE SPIRITUALITY WITHIN
THE PROTECTIVE WALLS OF STRENGTH AND COMMON SENSE.
AT ITS CENTRE IS THE YONI, THE FEMALE CREATIVE SYMBOL,
HELD LOVINGLY WITHIN THE LOTUS OF ENLIGHTENMENT.

1 Look at the square enclosure with its double-buttressed walls. It is deeply set within the spiritual – the outer circle and the lotus, both of which suggest purity. The square is the foundation that grounds us and prevents us from losing touch with the eternal truth.

2 Enter the lotus and let the lotus enter you. Meditating upon this mandala, you absorb all the energies and essences of the eternal creative feminine principle, which brings us into the physical world and at the same time gives us the gift of intuitive wisdom.

"For a woman is the everlasting field in which the self is born."

The Mahabharata (*c*.400 BC–*c*.AD 200)

THE HOLY GRAIL

FOR AN ARTHURIAN KNIGHT THE HOLY GRAIL MEANT
SELF-KNOWLEDGE, REDEMPTION, IMMORTALITY. HERE THE GRAIL
IS AT THE CENTRE OF THE ROUND TABLE, SURROUNDED BY THE
HELMETS OF THE KING AND SIX OF HIS KNIGHTS.

1 Look at the sword in the stone, which only the future king can remove. True meditation pulls the sword from the stone, as the physical world becomes subordinate to the spiritual.

2 Recognize that the king is a symbol of yourself. The knights around you are your personal qualities. See yourself as inwardly protected by armour and magic shields.

3 Lastly, feel worthy to approach the Grail, which is empty yet at the same time full of love. Imagine yourself holding the Grail and feeling its transforming power.

"I searched for God and found only myself.
I searched for myself and found only God."

Sufi proverb

CONFRONTING THE MINOTAUR

THE MINOTAUR, A BULL-LIKE CREATURE THAT LIVED IN A
LABYRINTH ON THE ISLAND OF CRETE, STANDS FOR ALL OUR
INNER DEMONS — ATTACHMENTS, FEARS, FAILINGS IN LOVE.
THROUGH MEDITATION WE CAN TAME THE MONSTER.

1 Think of the Minotaur as a source of
negative energy that you need to defeat.
As you enter the maze you unroll a
red thread from a spool: this is your
connection with the world of safety,
your knowledge that the Minotaur can
never really harm you.

2 Trace your way through the confusion
of many turnings — you are moving
deeper and deeper into the depths of
your being.

3 When at last you reach the centre,
you find that the Minotaur is already
harmless. What took courage initially
was facing the truth about yourself.

4 Now take the mandala into your mind
— maze, thread, bull and all. Dwell upon
it as the image of your spiritual heroism.

*"It is not because things are difficult that we do not dare,
it is because we do not dare that they are difficult."*

Seneca (*c.*4 BC–AD 65)

CELTIC DRAGONS

THE FIRE-BREATHING DRAGON IS FEARFUL AND POWERFUL,
BUT IN THIS MANDALA THE DRAGON'S POWER IS POURED
INTO THE ENDLESS KNOT OF SPIRITUAL PERFECTION.
EARTH AND SPIRIT BLEND IN COSMIC HARMONY.

1 Look at the fire that issues from the four dragons' heads at the top and bottom of the mandala. This is the physical energy of nature, which can become transmuted into spiritual energy. The fire forms a circle – its spiritual character is endless.

2 Now rest your eyes on the dragons' bodies transformed by spirit into an endless knot of eternal perfection.

Matter passes into spirit, which purifies it and enfolds it within an all-embracing cosmic harmony – giving birth to the "pearl of great price" in the mandala's centre.

3 Let the mandala become the centre of your awareness and allow the opposites of matter and spirit to blend together, to manifest the wholeness that is our essential nature.

"Accept whatever happens and let your spirit move freely."

Zhuangzi (c.369–c.286 BC)

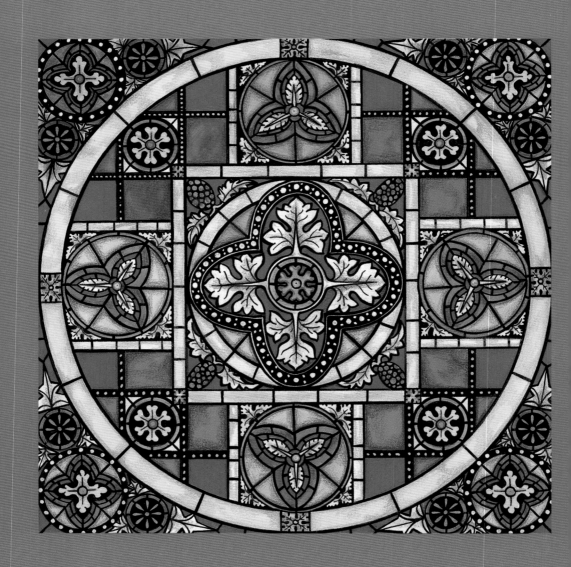

A STAINED-GLASS WINDOW

THE BEAUTY OF STAINED GLASS IS A GIFT OF SUNLIGHT —
ITS IMAGES, LIKE OURSELVES, WOULD BE LIFELESS WITHOUT THE SUN.
THIS MANDALA EVOKES THE PEACE OF A CHURCH OR TEMPLE
AND REJOICES IN THE SUN'S RADIANCE.

1 See the trefoils and quatrefoils of the design as symbolic of nature — the universe of infinite forms. The subject of the window is the harmony of the natural world, shown by leaves, flowers and bunches of berries.

2 Now start to see the pure design taking form as an actual window, which you are observing from the inside of a sacred building. Appreciate its artistry and workmanship.

3 Lastly, imagine that the window is lit from behind by bright sunlight. All the colours glow beautifully. The window has become a perfect symbol of nature animated by spirit and, at the same time, of human creativity animated by spiritual wisdom. As you draw the mandala deep into your mind, recognize that it reflects the essence of your true self.

"Truth and morning become light with time."

Ethiopian proverb

TIME AND THE UNIVERSE

THINKING ABOUT THE NATURE OF TIME CAN PRODUCE
CONFUSION, EVEN DESPAIR. FORGETTING THE CLOCK AND
SEEING TIME AS THE ETERNAL FLOW OF THE UNIVERSE
IS A REASSURING AND REFRESHING VISUAL MEDITATION.

1 Identify the elements of the mandala: time as a flow, the river changeless yet endlessly changing; the seasons; the movements of the stars, Earth, sun and moon; the four symbols of butterfly (briefer life than ours), tree (longer life than ours), spiral (infinite time) and Möbius strip (infinite space).

2 Still holding the mandala in your field of view, imagine all the separate meanings of these different aspects of time dissolving into the great river, the flow of the cosmos.

3 Feel yourself entering the great river of time, interfusing with its flow: the river is within you and you are within the river. The mandala is a drop of water, one of an infinite number of such drops. Relax into the endlessness of time and space.

"Every instant of time is a pinprick of eternity."

Marcus Aurelius (AD 120–180)

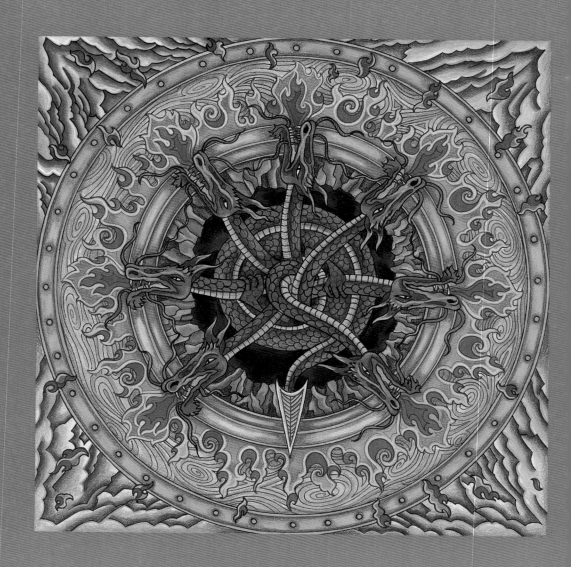

DRAGON ENERGY

THE DRAGON IS THE PARADOX OF BEING — LIGHT AND DARK,
CREATION AND DESTRUCTION, MALE AND FEMALE, AND THE
UNIFYING FORCE OF THESE OPPOSITES. THE DRAGON'S FIRE
IS THE PRIMAL ENERGY OF THE PHYSICAL WORLD.

1 Look at the mandala's seven-headed dragon and imagine its overwhelming, invincible power. Trace this power in the ring of flames. Nothing more awesome can be imagined in all the universe.

2 The seven heads symbolize the mystical number of the cosmos. They are the sum of the number of divinity (three) and the number of humankind (four).

3 Finally, concentrate on the knot of dragons' necks at the centre of the mandala. This is where all contradictions are resolved.

"The phantasmal is the bridge to the real."

Sufi saying

SRI YANTRA

THIS IS A SIMPLIFIED VERSION OF THE SACRED HINDU
SRI YANTRA. THE SRI YANTRA'S PATTERN OF INTERLINKING
TRIANGLES HAS A COMPELLING MYSTIC BEAUTY, REPRESENTING
THE TIMELESS CREATIVITY OF THE UNIVERSE.

1 Focus on the centre of the mandala and its opposing sets of triangles – these represent the male and female principles which in their fusion give rise to creation.

2 Now turn your attention to the geometry surrounding the image. Consider the equal-armed cross, whose elements represent the created cosmos, and the circle, denoting spiritual perfection.

3 Contemplate the central point of the Sri Yantra, which is called the *bindu*. This is the source of all creation. And your own mind, as it absorbs this yantra into itself, is unfolding from this transcendental, creative source. like everything else in the cosmos, past, present and future.

*"We meditate upon that divine sun, the true light
of the shining ones. May it illuminate our minds."*

The Gayatri Verse of the Vedas (*c.*5000 BC)

THE WORLD'S WEATHER

THE WEATHER IS A SYMBOL OF ENDLESS CHANGE. IT OFFERS
A LESSON IN ACCEPTANCE: IF WE FIND IT DIFFICULT TO ACCEPT
THE WEATHER REGARDLESS OF ANY PLANS WE HAVE MADE,
WE HAVE A LONG WAY TO GO IN OUR SPIRITUAL JOURNEY.

1 Look at the sun, which is shown in each of the four corners of this mandala. It is always there, driving life's energies, even when obscured by cloud. In the same way, our identity and our spirit are unaltered by shifts of fortune.

2 Now concentrate on the mandala's depiction of clouds, rain, rainbows, snow and rough seas. All this weather belongs to one vast self-regulating global system, which the mandala as a whole symbolizes.

3 Lastly, focus on the central point of the mandala – the still source of the endless streams of energy that bring all weathers and all other changes into the cosmos. This is the energy from which we are made. Take the mandala deep into your mind where that energy finds its still centre.

"Love is the wind, the tide, the waves, the sunshine."

Henry David Thoreau (1817–1862)

CAUSE AND EFFECT

IT IS SAID THAT WHEN A BUTTERFLY FLAPS ITS WINGS IN JAPAN,
IT CAUSES A HURRICANE IN LOUISIANA. TO SEE THAT ALL THE
WORLD'S EVENTS ARE CONNECTED IS TO UNDERSTAND THAT WE
SHOULD ALL TAKE RESPONSIBILITY FOR OUR ACTIONS.

1 Look at the three interconnected gear wheels. They are an obvious form of cause and effect.

2 Now look at the butterfly, whose wings flap metaphorically to create a storm on the other side of the world. This is cause producing effects invisibly. Such unseen connections occur throughout existence.

3 Focus on the mandala as a whole: its asymmetrical form around an inner wheel conceals the harmony of the cosmos. In the same way, any imbalances in our own lives conceal the unified whole of the spirit.

4 Finally, contemplate the hub of the central wheel. Take it deep into your consciousness and become aware that all life revolves around a still central point.

"Through what is near, one understands what is far away."

Hsun-tzu (c.300–238 BC)

THE ENDLESS KNOT

WELL KNOWN AS A CELTIC SYMBOL, BUT WITH PARALLELS
IN HINDU, BUDDHIST AND CHINESE TRADITIONS, THE ENDLESS
KNOT REPRESENTS INFINITY, THE ENDLESS FLOW OF TIME AND
MOVEMENT, AND THE JOURNEY OF THE PILGRIM.

1 Become aware of the endless knot in the mandala – the elaborately interlaced thread without a starting point. See this as a transcendental state beyond the material world. Visually trace the thread to satisfy yourself that it has no end.

2 Focus on the central cross within the circle – a symbol of the physical (the cross) fused with the spiritual (the circle).

3 Now let these two images – the encircled cross and the endless knot – enter your mind as a single expression of the eternal truth of existence: all existence is time-bound, but ultimately it rests timelessly within the divine or eternal spirit. Relax in this timelessness throughout your meditation.

"The end and the beginning of being are unknown. We see only the form in between. So what cause is there for grief?"

The Bhagavad Gita (*c.*5th century BC)

ARCHES OF THE HEAVENS

THE DOME OF A TEMPLE OR CHURCH IS OFTEN MANDALA-
LIKE WHEN SEEN FROM BELOW — A PATTERN MADE UP OF
THE ARCHES OF WINDOWS AND CRISS-CROSSING ROOF SUPPORTS.
THE RESULTING VIEW, OF COURSE, IS HEAVENWARD.

1 Pick out the main features of the mandala – the view directly upward into an elaborate dome. The three-dimensional geometry is complex, but don't try to decipher each decorative or structural element, just absorb the basic architecture, and the four decorative flower motifs.

2 Imagine sunlight passing through the windows of the dome and bringing it to life, in the same way that sunlight gives life to living beings.

3 Think of the image as a two-dimensional pattern again, and take it deep into your mind – you are now contemplating the heavens and the life-affirming light of divinity. You are peacefully at prayer – although you are asking for nothing.

"Geometry is an abstraction of beauty.
Add light and this beauty becomes spiritual."

Modern meditation from San Francisco

A PAGODA

THE PAGODA ADDS A SPIRITUAL DIMENSION TO THE JAPANESE
GARDEN, DEPICTING OUR ASCENT TO HEAVENLY BLISS THROUGH
STAGES OF ENLIGHTENMENT. THIS MANDALA ALSO SYMBOLIZES
THE BALANCE BETWEEN NATURE AND ARTIFICE.

1 View the pagoda as a succession of separate temples, one built on top of another. This is the triumph of art over formlessness, yet its purpose is not to aggrandize humanity but to assert the vitality of the spirit.

2 Notice that the pagoda has open sides. The building is a meeting-point of emptiness and solidity.

3 Contemplate the uppermost level, with its pointed roof. This symbolizes spirit – the crowning glory of the created world. Whatever stage you are at on your journey, you can see your destination clearly. All the ladders on which you will climb are already present and there for the finding.

"Logic will get you from A to B. Imagination will take you everywhere."

Albert Einstein (1879–1955)

THE WORLD TREE

WITH ITS ROOTS AROUND THE EARTH AND ITS BRANCHES
IN THE HEAVENS, THE WORLD TREE SYMBOLIZES OUR ABILITY
TO TRANSCEND OUR HUMBLE ORIGINS IN THE DENSE REALM
OF MATTER AND ASCEND TO HEAVENLY BLISS.

1 Contemplate the world tree, so vast that its canopy stretches over day and night. The tree's fruits are the good things given to us by the divine – the harvest of virtues, including love, compassion, peace and self-awareness. In your knowledge of this tree, and of its fruits, you are immensely privileged. You are aware that, as long as you keep this knowledge in your heart, you will be fulfilling your true destiny.

2 Sense the essence of the world tree rising through the trunk and branches as you bring them deep into your mind, and through the channels of your heart and spirit. This vital essence is both material and spiritual.

3 Understand that if a branch falls to the ground, the tree still stands. In the same way your spiritual essence is eternal, whatever accidents befall your body.

*"When the wind of pure thought rustles among its leaves,
the World Tree whispers the name of the divine."*

Modern meditation from Germany

PALACE OF THE GODS

TRADITIONAL MANDALAS WERE OFTEN SEEN AS DIAGRAMS
OF THE PALACE OF THE GODS. THIS MODERN VERSION SHOWS
A PLAN OF THE PALACE AND SIDE-ON VIEWS OF EIGHT
PAVILIONS. THE PALACE IS BOTH THE COSMOS AND THE SELF.

1 In your mind enter the sacred palace gardens, as defined by the outer circle of the mandala. Here you are outside time and space. The large circle and the smaller ones inside it generate a spiritual atmosphere.

2 Think of the four pavilions in the outer wall of the palace as the domain of earth, air, fire and water. All four elements dwell in the mandala, in the cosmos and in your own self.

The fifth element, ether or spirit, has its own inner enclosure. Enter the inner square now. Once inside, you are able to transcend Earthly barriers (the concentric square walls) and bathe in the sacred fountain.

3 The fountain flows inside you endlessly, the life-force that sustains your being. It is blessed by the divine, and brings infinite peace to your spirit.

"God is consciousness that pervades the entire universe
of the living and the non-living."

Sri Ramakrishna (1836–1886)

HEALING MANDALAS

THE MANDALAS THAT FOLLOW ARE OF THREE KINDS. THE FIRST
TEN (PAGES 180–211) GIVE YOU ROUTES TOWARD YOUR STILL
CENTRE. YOU CAN USE THEM TO DRAW EMOTIONAL AND SPIRITUAL
SUSTENANCE FROM WITHIN, BUILDING SELF-ESTEEM AND CREATIVITY.
THE SECOND TEN (212–245) ENCOURAGE YOU TO ADDRESS AND
EXPLORE THE RELATIONSHIPS IN YOUR LIFE, FINDING NEW WAYS OF
NURTURING YOURSELF THROUGH PEACE-MAKING, FORGIVENESS AND
ACCEPTING ADVERSITY. AND THE LAST TEN (246–279) WILL HELP
YOU TO FIND THE STRENGTH AND RESOURCEFULNESS TO OVERCOME
ILLNESS, LOSS AND LONELINESS SO THAT, LIKE THE PHOENIX RISING
FROM THE ASHES OF ITS FORMER SELF, YOU MAY EVEN EMERGE FROM
TIMES OF DIFFICULTY REJUVENATED IN HEART AND MIND.

"I saw that everything, all paths I had been following, all steps I had taken, were leading back to a single point — namely, to the mid-point. It became increasingly plain to me that the mandala is the centre. It is the exponent of all paths. It is the path to the centre, to individuation ... I knew that in finding the mandala as an expression of the self I had attained what was for me the ultimate."

C. G. Jung (1875–1961)

A PATH TO WHOLENESS

A mandala is a symbolic picture or pattern used in meditation. Its various motifs, its colours and its geometry are specifically designed to bring about inner focus and inner peace. Mandalas most often take the form of a circle – a shape that represents the self, the Earth, the sun, the cosmos and the state of wholeness that is the ultimate aim of mandala meditation. By taking this path we move toward a state of completeness and a realization of our true nature, which, like the circle of the mandala, is boundless and perfect. Experiencing such a deep sense of unity is immensely healing.

The unique pressures of modern living make the need for healing more prevalent now than ever. As we work longer hours, commute further and often don't take enough time to eat healthily, exercise or unwind, so the statistics for stress-related illness rise. The high expectations that we set ourselves strain our physical, mental and emotional resources, and may lead to physical symptoms, relationship problems or a generalized sense of lack of fulfilment. All are messages we should take notice of and act upon.

Fortunately, body and mind have an immense capacity for self-regeneration. And if we slow down and dive within, we can create space for this to develop. Try this experiment. Clench your fist and see what happens. You probably feel tense and closed-in. Then relax your hand. Do you feel more open, more receptive? The same principle applies to the mind: when it is stressed your body will feel tense, but when your mind is quiet, the body follows suit, relaxing in a way that allows our innate healing processes to begin their work.

It is interesting to see what happens when we make a space for our thoughts, and then within this space refuse to dwell on the negative. Inevitably, anxieties or other negative thoughts will invade our space, but we have the option to just let them drift away, out of our minds. They can only stay if we allow them to. Positive thoughts, on the other hand, may be encouraged. This "space", as we have called it, could simply be the backdrop of consciousness, the mind itself. But it could also be the mandala on which you meditate.

In a mandala, we generate an arena that allows only positive thoughts into its circle. It isn't that we are concentrating hard upon a task: the process is more open than that. It's more that we have created a filter, so that only positive thoughts are allowed to linger, while negative ones are ignored. The positive thoughts arise, in the first place, from the energies of the mandala's symbolism. We open ourselves to the influence of the mandala, and allow our minds to focus lightly on its forms and symbols.

Healing begins at a profound level that we cannot control consciously. It might feel spontaneous and immediate, like a cog slipping into place. Or it might evolve over time. Mandala meditation allows you to encourage healing at a pace that is right for you. By setting aside as little as fifteen minutes every day to look at a mandala, you will take the first steps on a journey away from anxiety and stress toward the increased balance, optimism and freedom that come from reconnecting with your inner resources and gaining a fresh perspective on life's challenges.

ENERGY HEALING

To restore equilibrium to our often unbalanced lifestyles, many of us turn to complementary therapies such as homeopathy, acupuncture, reiki and colour therapy. Although these therapies adopt different methods, they all take as their starting point the principle that there are energies at work within the body. Imbalances within our energy system, if left untreated, can manifest as symptoms of illness. But harmony can be restored by therapies using subtle adjustments whose workings cannot be explained by Western science.

In homeopathy, "new vibrations" are introduced to our energy systems in the form of pills or tinctures that include minute amounts of a substance shaken at high speed to increase its vibrational force. In acupuncture treatments, fine needles are inserted into energy points on the body to undo blockages in our "meridians" – the channels through which energy circulates. In reiki, a healer channels energy through his or her hands.

It is beyond the scope of this book to argue that mandala meditation can heal in similar ways by bringing harmony to our energy systems – although such a view would have its adherents. However, the case in favour of mandala meditation can be made modestly, without migrating to the outer fringes of the mind-body-spirit movement. The influence of the mind on the state of the body is well established: think of placebos, of the physical symptoms of stress, of the way in which we can train ourselves to overcome phobias and anxieties, and of the proven power of hypnosis.

Buddhists sometimes use the analogy of rust, which comes from iron, yet can destroy iron. In the same way, a negative state of mind can hasten the destructive power of illness; while conversely, positive feelings may provide a bulwark against many ailments. Meditation can release tension and prime the mind to allow the body's immunity defences to work at full strength. No one loses anything by trying.

THE POWER OF MEDITATION

There are many forms of meditation. You can observe or count your breath (in, out, in, out) or gaze at a candle until you feel a sense of unity with the flame. In mantra meditation you repeat a word or phrase designed to positively influence both your mind and body. And in mandala meditation you let your gaze settle on a circular image. In all forms, the ultimate aim is to dissolve differences between you and the object of meditation: to close the gap that makes you feel separate.

Any form of meditation has enormous benefits for physical, mental *and* emotional health. The psychological effects of meditation include a reduction in anxiety, moodiness and depression, improved memory and self-esteem, and increased emotional stability and happiness. Physically, meditation has been shown in numerous studies to lower blood pressure, enhance the immune system and relax the body, leading to a healthier heart-rate. On a more spiritual level, meditation enhances your perception and intuition, and helps to open up a deep well of inner wisdom and a sense of higher connection.

Meditation allows us to look at what is going on in both our minds and our bodies. It gives us the space to become conscious of our unhelpful mental and physical habits and to counteract them when we need to. It is recommended by more and more doctors as a tool to enhance and speed up the healing process, especially for certain medical conditions, such as high blood pressure. The method combines well with conventional treatment and has no adverse side effects or contraindications.

MANDALA MEDITATION FOR EVERYONE

Mandalas are particularly broad-ranging meditation tools. They can be used by beginners and experienced practitioners of meditation alike, and there is no need to undergo a period of tutoring or self-discipline. Many other forms of meditation require regular practice to train the mind, but anyone can simply sit with a mandala and soon begin to gain benefits. Even without understanding their symbolism, the images contained within a mandala speak directly to the unconscious, producing an experience of profound harmony and sense of oneness with the spiritual forces they represent.

Mandalas are designed so that your eye and attention are naturally drawn to certain areas in the structure and then progressively led through other imagery – it can feel like taking a relaxed walk on a sunny day. You can benefit from spending just ten minutes with a mandala, but if you allow this to extend to fifteen or thirty minutes at a sitting, you will experience the positive effects more profoundly. Soon you will notice that you feel more relaxed, your concentration is sharper, and your thoughts and responses more effective. In this state of underlying calm, any irritation or disappointment that comes along is less likely to seem important, and it will therefore become easier to maintain equanimity.

It can be useful to keep a journal after mandala meditation. Note any thoughts and issues, reflections and insights that come to light. Sometimes the healing process involves recognizing patterns that you might previously have denied – simple recognition can allow you to start making changes.

MORE THAN MEDITATION

Healing is synonymous with "becoming whole" – attaining a state of internal and external harmony. To heal, we must bring imbalances in the mind and heart back into a state of equilibrium, which in turn has a positive effect on the body. However, mandala meditation is about more than this: it also makes us more whole by strengthening our connection with our essential nature and with the source of all things. As the power of our practice increases we should be able to merge our consciousness with the mandala, actualizing within ourselves the qualities it represents.

The pioneering psychologist Carl Jung (1875–1961) asserted that mandalas are a key to personal transformation because they represent "an archetype of wholeness". Through the power of their symbolism, they allow us to apprehend the manifold aspects of the cosmos (the macrocosm) reflected in each of us (the microcosm), albeit unknowingly. Contemplating a mandala expands our limited perspective to show us the interconnectedness of everything in the universe. This makes us feel more complete and gives an insight into our spiritual nature. We free ourselves from unhelpful ways of thinking that prevent our inner growth.

If we consciously use this new way of seeing to cultivate inner harmony during testing times, we begin to react more constructively to everyday stresses. This healing benefits all areas of life – from relationships with our partner, friends and family to our career and our creative projects – and filters through to create well-being in the body as well as in the mind and heart.

MANDALAS IN DIFFERENT TRADITIONS

Humankind has created mandala-like designs since earliest times, across different cultures and faith traditions, with whatever materials have been to hand. Our distant ancestors left marks on the walls of caves, traced patterns in sand, placed stones in sacred alignments, and constructed great circular tombs such as those at Newgrange in Ireland and Maeshowe in Scotland. More readily associated with meditation are the Eastern designs that are now familiar in the West. But creating mandalas is a *living* tradition, whether the images are pixellated on a computer or hand-wrought onto paper, silk, canvas or sand.

Mandalas have always been viewed as a path to enlightenment – a method by which our mind can connect with the life-force of the universe and so attain liberation. In Indian, Tibetan and Chinese versions they traditionally depict complex cultural symbols, sometimes including deities, to express in pictorial form the profound nature of universal reality. The Tibetan Kalachakra deity, to take one important example, lies at the centre of a mandala that is considered to be the god's sacred palace and is used in Tantric spiritual initiation rites as well as for healing practices. The centre where he sits is the matrix: the "all" from which everything manifests. After the rites have been performed, the elaborate mandala, executed in coloured sands made up of precious stones finely crushed, is swept away as a lesson in impermanence.

Large-scale "mandalas" formed by alignments of stones in the landscape may possibly have a global purpose beyond the spiritual healing of the

community. Like giant acupuncture needles, they may seek to optimize the energy of the planet, as they tend to be sited on powerful earth-energy points along meridians crisscrossing the land. They also connect with the universe as astronomic observatories, their alignments charting the movements of heavenly bodies.

The Native American medicine wheel, a circle of rocks with radiating spokes made from smaller stones, tracks astronomical alignments and is also used for healing and teaching purposes. Some tribes divide the wheel into sections according to the cardinal points: north is often identified with adulthood, south with childhood, west with adolescence and east with death and rebirth. The wheel can also be symbolic in terms of the elements, colours and races of humankind.

Indigenous Australian sand mandalas invoke a time of creation, known as the Dreamtime, when the laws of the universe came into being, strengthening the people's connections with the land.

The Indian science of Vastu uses a giant mandala to bring new buildings and even town-planning in line with terrestrial and cosmic forces, thereby harnessing positive energy and healing. The Dogon people in Mali, Africa, construct their homes in the shape of a mandala that echoes the cosmos: the dwellings are built in pairs to represent Heaven and Earth, while the ground is dug in spirals to follow the energy of the earth. Much smaller domestic mandalas, such as Native American dreamcatchers and medicine shields and Chinese feng-shui diagrams, bring potent healing energy and protection right into the heart of the home.

Left: A Native American medicine wheel in Arizona. The circular forms and internal structures of medicine wheels reflect complex astrological alignments and, just like mandalas, can be used as tools for meditation.

MAPS OF WELL-BEING

A mandala can be thought of as a map that leads us to a tranquil inner state – to what Carl Jung called "a safe refuge of inner reconciliation and wholeness". Along the way we glimpse different aspects of our multi-faceted psyche, which we may not have been aware of previously. As with any route-map, the mandala has a starting-point from which we take our first step on the journey toward wholeness. Liberated from the everyday constraints of space and time, we embark from here on our inner adventure. Traditionally, the initial point of focus is a dot at the centre of the circle, from which the eye travels outward; however, with some mandalas we may start at the outer rim, from which we move inward. A mandala's central focal point is known as the *bindu*, a Sanskrit word meaning "drop". It is helpful to imagine this as a safe place of stillness, where you can rediscover your true self and open up to the possibilities contained in the mandala. Once you connect with the energy of this point, you can experience it anywhere in the mandala.

From the *bindu*, the mandala map opens out like the petals of a rose to reveal multiple layers of reality. Each motif represents a different aspect of your psyche as well as some aspect within the cosmos. Resting your gaze on the motifs one by one, or all together in a single overview, leads you on a twofold voyage inward to the heart of the self and outward to explore the cosmos. Once you are in a relaxed state of mind, moving your eyes slowly over the symbols of the mandala relaxes you further. It also stimulates a blossoming that begins deep within and spreads all through your being. You are well placed now to allow the opposites within yourself to be harmonized and the healing energies of the design to exert their benign influence. Slowing down and penetrating deeper into wordless understanding, you discover the real you. Remember that the insights that follow mandala meditation are unique to you and reflect the discoveries made in the course of your inward adventure.

MANDALAS AND THE MIND

The symmetries, repetitions and contrasts of mandala patterns create a hypnotic effect that can cause changes in the rhythms of your brainwaves. This is nothing for anyone to be worried about: you experience this simply as a subtle shift in perspective and a sensation of greater serenity. As in all forms of meditation, contemplating a mandala settles the mind into first an Alpha and then a Theta state (as explained in the adjacent column). This has proven benefits for mind and body, from a reduction in heart and pulse rates and easier breathing to strengthened immunity.

Beta brainwave rhythm (30–40 HZ) Corresponds with a state of heightened alertness and concentration.

Alpha brainwave rhythm (7–12 HZ) Associated with a state of relaxation. In this state, your ability to visualize and to be creative is stimulated.

Theta brainwave rhythm (4–7 HZ) At the fringes of consciousness, this state of being nourishes intuition and memory. It also encourages insight and deep healing.

Delta brainwave rhythm (0–4 HZ) Correlates with a state of deep sleep.

SYMBOLS OF THE UNCONSCIOUS

Jungian psychology identifies several layers of consciousness. First, there is the individual's waking consciousness (thoughts, memories and perceptions) and his or her personal unconscious (dreams and forgotten memories). Then there is what might be called the "collective consciousness": the beliefs, perceptions and experiences common to everyone. Finally, and most interestingly, there is the collective unconscious: a shared, cross-cultural collection of archetypes, or universal images, that carry underlying symbolic meaning. The archetypes are thought to be present at the deepest levels of the "self", but most of us are only ever aware of a few of them – they may surface in dreams or

KEY ELEMENTS OF A MANDALA

The most important elements of a mandala's form are designed to work together to bring about a change in consciousness and, ultimately, a harmony of mind and body.

Bindu The central "seed" of the mandala is an intense concentration of energy, and a starting point for your inner exploration. It may be seen as the bottomless well of the self.

Circle Symbolizes the whole, and spiritual perfection. It can also represent the state of completeness that meditation fosters.

Square Shows the physical world and directions: north, south, east and west. Ground yourself here as you bring about inner transformation.

Perimeter The energy of the mandala is contained by this outer rim, which also allows your mind to work within familiar boundaries.

in creative work in various media. Of interest to practitioners of meditation are those particular archetypes – for example, certain deities and animals – that appear in mandalas.

Our drive as human beings, according to Jungian thought, is to experience a state of "individuation" – of becoming whole within ourselves. Meditating on a mandala helps us toward individuation because it allows us to explore and apprehend many aspects of the self – all those elements (including the archetypes of the collective unconscious) that we don't even know we have within us – and to bring them into focus. Let us take just two examples. Jung identifies the Anima, which is the feminine image within a male psyche, and the Animus, which is the masculine image within a female psyche. Meditating on the Anima or Animus in a mandala can help to attune you to the complementary gender within yourself, and all its qualities of compassion and intuition (Anima) and action and decisiveness (Animus).

It can be helpful to think about the images within a mandala as we think about the motifs in dreams. When we dream, we journey into our personal unconscious, but also into the collective unconscious, which is why dream symbols sometimes seem to express a universal language. In dreams, as in meditation, we are in the realm of intuition, not reason. We respond to images in ways that by-pass our faculties of reason. We may later intellectualize the experience, but what matters is our direct response to the power of symbols – at subconscious levels of the self. It is here that the healing energies of mandalas are effective.

HEALING WITH SUBTLE ENERGY

In order to understand a little more about how mandalas can bring about positive change, it is useful to learn about the force-field of subtle energy, known as an aura, which is thought to surround all living things. Some healers literally see this intangible "body" of energy as interpenetrating layers of subtly glowing colours, which follow the body's contours and reveal information about your health, emotions and spiritual development: the fine web of the aura

CHAKRA ASSOCIATIONS

Each chakra, or subtle energy centre, is linked to a part of the body and presides over a range of emotional, intellectual and spiritual responses.

Root chakra Located around the base of the spine, at the perineum, this chakra is associated with survival, security and instinct.

Sacral chakra Found just above the pubic bones, this chakra presides over sexuality, reproduction and creativity.

Solar-plexus chakra Felt just above the navel, this chakra governs energy, drive and motivation.

Heart chakra At the centre of the chest, level with the heart, this chakra relates to loving emotions such as kindness.

Throat chakra Sensed around the hollow at the base of the throat, this chakra is linked to communication and healthy self-expression.

Third-eye chakra Found at the centre of the forehead, this is the mind's eye, where you relate to your intuition and visionary capacity.

Crown chakra Felt at the crown of the head, this is the highest chakra, which presides over consciousness and spiritual insight.

is said to become distorted or torn around areas of disease, and the colours are thought to vary in luminosity according to your emotional state. The deep breathing that mandala meditation promotes is thought to strengthen the aura, making its colours appear more vibrant – a sign of good health.

Within the energy of the aura lie the seven major chakras (see box, opposite), centres of subtle energy visualized as wheels that gather life-force and distribute it to the various realms of the body, emotions and intellect. How smoothly our chakras function determines how well we feel in our physical body, how successful our relationships are and how much inner peace we are able to enjoy.

Each chakra governs a particular set of physical, mental and emotional processes, which becomes more refined as we move up the chakra system: for example, our instinct for security and survival is ruled by the root, or base, chakra, situated around the perineum, while spiritual insight is determined at the highest chakra, sited at the crown of the head.

Because the colours, shapes and many of the archetypal images found in mandalas are linked with particular chakras, you may find yourself drawn to a mandala because you have a specific, often unconscious, need for healing in the realm of the body ruled by that chakra. As your gaze rests upon the mandala, the chakra is stimulated to rebalance the flow of energy to its corresponding parts of the body, emotions or intellect, improving your health and the way in which you can respond to problems caused by the world and people around you.

THE POWER
OF COLOUR

Colours have an impact on our emotions and moods. It is hard to sustain the case that these associations are necessarily universal, as some of them are culturally determined: for example, in certain countries the hue of mourning is not black but white. Even so, there are numerous equivalences that can be taken as standard.

By opting for a certain colour, in our dress or in our environment, we can go some way toward lifting a bad mood or increasing our energy levels. How many times have you walked through a wood carpeted with bluebells or witnessed a vibrant orange sunset and not felt your spirits improve? Research has shown that colour choice may even be able to boost immunity or speed the recovery of hospital patients following an operation.

One of the first things that may draw us to a particular mandala is its palette of colours. By focusing on particular colours within the design during your meditation, you can open yourself to their beneficial energies.

What is at work here are the different wavelengths of light, which manifest as various colours. The waves become shorter as the seven colours of the rainbow move in a continuous spectrum from red at one end through orange, yellow, green, blue, and indigo to violet at the other end. Each vibration is said by energy healers to affect your aura by balancing the chakra with which that colour is associated (see box, opposite, for specific information on these links). You might find yourself drawn to colours in a mandala that relate to areas of the body or psyche that require healing most urgently.

COLOUR SYMBOLISM

The following colours have a particular energy profile and chakra association, alongside their traditional symbolism.

Red The colour of blood, red is energizing and warming. It can increase vitality, joy, passion and motivation. Connected with the root chakra, red stimulates the survival instinct, counters low energy and strengthens the organs of elimination. Too much can cause aggression.

Orange Traditionally the hue of fertility, love and splendour, orange brings upbeat, happy emotions. It is linked with the sacral chakra and used to stimulate creativity, positivity and sexual energy.

Yellow Although linked with treachery in China and elsewhere, this colour generally fosters cheerfulness and strengthens memory and intellect. It can also help to increase commitment. Yellow links with the solar-plexus chakra and is used to boost the digestive system, pancreas and adrenal glands.

Green Associated with growth, spring, youth and renewal, green has calming, harmonizing qualities, and can help to relieve anxiety and stress. It links with the heart chakra and is used to balance the immune system, lungs and heart. Green helps us to deal with issues of love, self-esteem and relationships with others.

Blue Cooling and soothing, blue encourages a sense of tranquillity. It is also symbolic of infinity, devotion, faith and chastity. Linked with the throat chakra, blue is used to ease throat ailments and unblock problems with communication.

Indigo A spiritually uplifting hue, indigo helps to calm the mind and promote restful sleep. This colour is associated with the third-eye chakra, stimulates the pineal gland and promotes inspiration.

Violet This colour fosters spiritual refinement and insight. Linked with the crown chakra, it stimulates the pituitary gland, hormones and growth.

SYMBOLS
OF HEALING

Images are more ancient and universal
than alphabets, words or writing, for
they tap into our collective unconscious
(see page 162). Throughout history and
all across the world they have been used
to express feelings, provoke reactions, tell
stories and embody philosophies –
as well as to heal and increase a sense of
connection with nature and with our
spiritual source.

Although the meanings of symbols
vary to some extent from culture to
culture, our shared experience as human
beings – principally an experience of
nature and of the human life-cycle –
has generated a universal language of
symbolism. Because motifs such as a
tree, a flower, water, fire, sun and moon
speak to people intuitively, regardless of
race or creed, they offer great potential

for exploration in healing. It is these
signs that form the basis of many of the
mandalas in this book.

In addition there is the symbolic
geometry of the mandala, and this too is
universal: the circle is universally endless,
the triangle always suggests a flame, the
square always signifies the created world.
Other, more culturally rooted symbols
used in these pages – the Egyptian Eye
of Horus, the Sanskrit *Om* symbol, the
I Ching hexagrams of China – have
an intrinsic beauty and long-lived
significance that endows them with a
universal potency.

On pages 170–179 you will find a
series of commentaries on many of the
symbols used in the mandalas. Further
information on specific symbols is given
in the meditations that accompany the
thirty mandalas in this chapter, and on
the feature pages (with quotations) that

punctuate these meditations. Each time you meditate on the mandalas, keep your mind open to the full range of possible interpretations. One image can carry a number of associations – the rose, for example, can stand for love, beauty and compassion. Your response to a motif at any moment will reflect not only your worldview, your cultural background and your knowledge, but also your changing moods. This aspect of variability adds depth to mandala meditation and enlarges its healing potential.

SYMBOLIC ARCHITECTURE

A church, a temple or a chapel can serve as a three-dimensional mandala, with symbolic geometry and motifs all around. Such buildings have healing potential for those who use them as a sanctuary for body, mind and spirit.

Dome Symbolically, the dome is either the cosmos or the heavens. Any light that enters is the light of spiritual wisdom.

Stupa This type of Buddhist temple is structured to symbolize the five elements. Its square base represents earth; its hemispherical dome, water; and its conical spire, fire. The crescent moon finial signifies air; its circular disk, space.

Cross The vertical and horizontal axes of a cross represent the potential for spirit and matter to meet, as well as the redemptive possibilities of human suffering.

Mesoamerican pyramid Some stepped temples in Central America are models of the cosmos. Often, the north side of their square plan represents the underworld; the south side, life and rebirth.

GEOMETRIC SHAPES

Geometry is a key element in mandala symbolism. The mind is drawn to geometric shapes, which, as objects of meditation, help to establish a positive framework for our thoughts. Free of explicit representational content, geometry has a purity that enables it to work well as a mental resting place. Yet at the same time, it can be rich in implications. It offers ways of visualizing, for example, the concept of eternity (the circle) or the interaction of spirit and flesh (the cross).

Circle In the circle, we experience perfect symmetry, integrity, unity and completeness, and beyond those qualities, a visual equivalent of eternity. In mandalas, the basic circle shape is emblematic of the spiritual, in contrast to the earthly square. As a ring, the endlessness of the circle signifies commitment: a promise never to falter. Interlocking circles make this promise mutual.

Spiral A common form in nature (think, for example, of a snail's shell or a whirlpool), the continuous curves of the spiral symbolize a cyclical and progressive continuity. The form suggests our inner growth as we move onward and inward in our wide-ranging explorations of our own consciousness. A solar symbol, the spiral has strong associations of latent power. It is also linked with the unfolding of time – including birth and death and the cyclic rhythms of the seasons. In Indian thought, kundalini is the coiled spiral of energy at the base of the human spine.

Central point The central point of a mandala, traditionally known in

Right: Spirals, often found in shells (this is a Moon Snail shell), may occur in mandalas.
They symbolize our deepening understanding as we spiral into our own inner selves.

Sanskrit as the *bindu*, stands for our own awareness as we start our meditation. Everything begins and ends with this dot, which is both seed and bud. It is the point at which the self recognizes its identity with the One.

Square This shape stands for Earth as opposed to Heaven, though it can also imply the solid, created universe as distinct from the transcendent creator, the One. The square also suggests a pause or breathing space.

Cross This is the most complex of all linear symbols. It is both the emblem of Christianity and a more ancient image of the cosmos reduced to its simplest terms – two intersecting lines indicating four directions, the cardinal points. The cross is also a simplification of the Tree of Life, its vertical axis suggesting spiritual ascension and its horizontal axis earthly life.

Triangle This ancient symbol of wisdom and spirit may suggest spiritual energy flowing into the physical world. Equilateral triangles in a mandala encourage in the viewer a reassuring sense of unity. The three points of a triangle reminds us of a trinity – humanity, God and spirit, or perhaps earth, sea and sky. (For interlocking triangles, see next entry.)

Star A star may be a five-pointed pentacle (comprising a continuous line) or a six-pointed hexagram (two interlocking triangles, one inverted in relation to the other). The pentacle, as the Star of Solomon, is a symbol of health and mystic harmony. The hexagram symbolizes union in duality (body/soul, male/female, and so on). More straightforwardly, a shining star, with alternating long and short points, is an auspicious sign and a spiritual centre.

NUMBER SYMBOLISM

The components of mandalas are often repeated, and when they are, there tends to be hidden symbolism in their numerical meaning. You might not consciously connect with a number and its symbolic significance as you meditate on a mandala, but often the number will feel relevant and carry weight.

1 A reminder of your singularity (your indivisible perfection) as well as of unity – the lack of differentiation between you and the cosmos.

2 Symbolizes duality, and also the division of the cosmos into opposites, such as male/female, light/dark, yin/yang and internal/external. The number may call you to balance and harmony.

3 The most positive of numbers, implying synthesis, growth, creativity.

4 Four components in a mandala may suggest stability, order, the Earth, justice. They can offer a reassuring sense of working within clearly defined boundaries.

5 Echoes the human form with four limbs, head, and five senses. The number may point to the power of individuality and spiritual aspirations.

6 Represents balance and symmetry, while doubling the creative energy of the number three.

7 A sacred, mystical and magical number, symbolizing cosmic and spiritual order, and the completion of a cycle or series (days of the week, number of chakras).

8 Can evoke a sensation of solidity, and doubles the qualities of the number four.

9 A triple triad, considered to be a very powerful number, symbolizing completion, fulfilment, perfection and the attainment of spiritual heights.

NATURE'S LEXICON

Nature is a source of inspiration and value. We treasure those phenomena of the cosmos that are independent of humankind.

In mandalas, the deeply symbolic associations of plants, and sometimes animals, speak to us at a level that transcends our cultural differences. To some extent, a tree or a flower has general significance related to nature's cycles, while animals tend to represent the Other, a self that is emphatically not our own. But when we consider individual families or species of plants or animals, a more individual symbolism comes into play – for example, the association of pine trees, in Japanese tradition, with longevity, or the cat, in Western tradition, with instinctive pliability and subtlety.

Trees With their roots in the soil and their branches in the sky, trees inhabit both Earthly and heavenly realms: they are antennae for spiritual energy from above, yet remain firmly anchored in the created world.

Flowers Though short-lived – a symbol of our impermanence – flowers remind us of the inner beauty that will flourish if we conduct ourselves well in thought and deed.

Animals Creatures, both real and mythical, can be read as elements of our instinctive nature – an antidote to over-sophistication yet dangerous if allowed to revert to bestial appetites.

Birds In mandalas, birds generally suggest transcendence. The dove is a familiar emblem of peace, purity, love, tenderness and hope. The eagle, soaring in the realm of spirit, and looking down on the world, evokes clarity of vision.

READING THE ELEMENTS

The Western tradition recognizes four elements – earth, fire, air and water – corresponding to the four seasons. In the Chinese tradition, however, there is also a fifth season, with its own element: ether, spirit or space. When your eye rests upon motifs that represent the elements or seasons in a mandala, you begin to tap into their energies, which can help to bring body and mind toward greater equilibrium in much the same way that spending time in nature is restorative.

Earth Usually represented as mountains, rocks, soil or grass, earth in a mandala reminds us of the material, practical part of our lives. It may allude to healing the body and issues to do with work and possessions. Earth is linked to the north and to winter, the season of recuperative withdrawal and dormancy.

Air Depicted as blowing leaves or clouds, air in a mandala stands for the mind, and the power of thought. Air is the medium of communication, which may be the clue to healing. This element is linked to the east and spring, a time of fresh growth and new beginnings.

Fire Flame-like motifs stand for fire, the source of spirit, inspiration and passion, as well as action and enthusiasm. Fire's healing action is cleansing and transformative: it destroys unwanted clutter, creating space for the new. Fire links to the south and summer, when energy is highest.

Water This ebbing and flowing element symbolizes the emotions. Often it takes a moving form: rivers, waterfalls, oceans, teardrops. Water shapes itself to the container that holds it, reminding us to be flexible. It is linked to the west and autumn, a time of gathering and preparation.

Ether Sometimes shown as the sky, ether urges us to look for the spiritual source, beyond form. Also, it is set at the hub of the wheel of the elements and seasons, which magnifies its healing potency.

COSMIC SYMBOLS

Images of heavenly bodies in mandalas remind us to expand our horizons from our own individual concerns by looking out toward the vast, awesome universe.

The cosmos makes us feel small when we contemplate its immeasurable magnitude, yet in fact this immensity is part of ourselves, and the cosmos is very much our home. By meditating on mandalas we can feel this sense of belonging even as we start more fully to comprehend the sublime vastness of the universe. Similarly, we are connected to all other people by a powerful bond of spirit. Our separateness is an illusion: we are deeply in harmony with – indeed, continuous with – everyone and everything. Mandalas reconnect us with this truth.

Sun, moon and stars help us to apprehend our connection with the cosmos by forming a bridge between cosmic reality and human experience. The sun is incomprehensibly distant yet directly controls the seasons. All physical energy comes from the sun, making it apt as a symbol of spiritual energy, an analogy for divinity itself. As the source of heat, the sun represents vitality, passion, courage and eternally renewed youth; as the source of light out of darkness, it symbolizes knowledge, intellect and truth personified. In most traditions the sun represents the male principle – though it was female in some regional mythologies, including Japanese. Emblems for the sun include the gold disk, the winged disk, the half-disk with rays, and the star, spiral, ring, wheel, swastika, heart, rosette, lotus, sunflower and chrysanthemum.

The moon, with its monthly phases, is emblematic of change and renewal in nature and in human life, as well as having connotations of mystic wisdom, intuition, the feminine, fertility, psychic regeneration, resurrection, immortality, and mutability. Graphically, the moon often appears in iconography as a waxing crescent, a propitious sign for the sowing of crops. Psychology links the satellite with subjectivity, the emotions and our shifting moods. In China the moon also suggests the completed family – an association that may be extended to cover the universal kinship of all human beings across the globe.

TRADITIONAL MANDALA SYMBOLISM

The following traditional figures can be found depicted in the mandalas that a lot of us are most familiar with: those of the Buddhist faith.

Healing Buddha Featured in diverse forms in different traditions, the Healing Buddha embodies the state of enlightenment, and liberation from the cycle of birth and rebirth. By gazing on him, we reconnect with our own Buddha-like nature, which is untroubled by the material world.

Tara In Tibet, Tara is the female embodiment of the Buddha and represents unconditional love and compassion. Green Tara and White Tara are the forms most called upon for healing. In China, Tara appears as Kuan Yin.

Bodhisattvas These figures are enlightened beings who have chosen to remain in the material world to relieve the suffering of their fellow creatures. They remind us that spiritual hope and comfort are there for us in times of need if only we can be receptive.

The stars, less precisely, suggest the ineffable wonder of creation, spiritual aspiration and the promise of transcendence. Supremacy, constancy, guidance, guardianship and vigilance are secondary associations, but more usually the general implication is simply the sublime beauty and goodness of the cosmos and the promise of a heavenly beyond. The time taken for a star's light to reach our eyes also makes us think of vast timescales – and, by extension, of eternity.

A pattern of stars, randomly or evenly sprinkled, underlines the suggestion of harmony – an eternal background to all Earth's turbulence and striving. Shooting stars, or comets, were thought to presage important events, and may appear in modern mandalas as emblems of fleeting epiphany – a sign of great things to come.

HUMAN AND HEAVENLY FORMS

Traditional mandalas often feature figures – especially deities (see page 177) and demons. Where the Buddha appears in a mandala, he reminds us of the enlightenment that may be attained by following his principles of detachment from cravings, extinction of desire, and the key principles of right thinking, right action, right speech, right effort, right awareness and right concentration. In the Tibetan Tantric tradition, the Buddha appears in female form as the goddess Tara, fount of unconditional love. Her protective action on behalf of all living beings is said to exceed that of a mother for her child. Green Tara is called upon in times of trouble and fear; White Tara, the "Mother of all Buddhas", is looked to as a source of compassion, purity, truth and unselfishness. Christians have their own equivalent of this feminine energy in the Virgin Mary.

In modern mandalas you might also encounter figures from the Greek and Roman pantheons – for example, Aphrodite or Venus for help in love or in creative pursuit; the centaur Chiron, tutor to gods and heroes, for healing inner and outer wounds; Mars for assertiveness; Mercury to foster communication.

HARMONY
IN DUALITY

Mandala designs often include motifs that suggest a harmonious balance of opposites – most commonly the Chinese yin-yang symbol of interdependence, which features black and white areas within a circle, divided by an S-shaped curve. Each area of the symbol includes a dot, or seed, of its opposite colour to show that the duality of light/dark, male/female, logic/intuition is not absolute: instead, there is a balanced dynamism, an interdependence of contrary forces within the cosmos. The yang contains the energy of the yin, and vice versa. Creative tension between the two generates change and motion, and gives texture and colour to our life's experiences.

Spiritual teachers tell us that physical dualities are simply diverse expressions of the One – the unity and completeness that are the ultimate creative force, symbolized in a mandala by its outer circle and its central miniature dot. By absorbing the entire mandala in a single gaze, we can attune ourselves to cosmic harmony and drink in the sense of deep peace and unity that provides the foundation-stone for healing.

SPIRAL OF LIFE

WE ARE ALL CHILDREN OF THE COSMOS. THE MOLECULES THAT
MAKE UP THE PHYSICAL SELF ARE FOUND UNIVERSALLY: WE ARE
ALL ONE. SENSING THE COSMIC LIFE-ENERGY WE SHARE ALLOWS
US TO BECOME MORE WHOLE. THIS IS THE ESSENCE OF HEALING.

1 Rest your gaze on the embryo in the protective egg at the centre of the mandala – a symbol of new life and potential. Feel cradled in the confidence that there are infinite possibilities for future growth.

2 Now let your eyes find the spirals of gold around the baby. Their shape is a reminder that life moves in cycles, and that we are all engaged in constant change and growth.

3 Next, focus on the twisting strands of DNA that define all the features of your unique self. Imagine some of these transforming into strands of pearls – or wisdom.

4 Finally, bathe in the vibrant blue of boundless space and inner potential, and trace the perfect circle enclosing this place of wonder. Feel no fear. You are safe here to express all the aspects of your true nature.

"Life is the soul's nursery –
its training place for the destinies of eternity."

William Makepeace Thackeray (1811–1863)

SELF IN THE COSMOS

EVERYTHING BEGINS WITH THE SELF. ALTHOUGH EACH OF US
IS BUT A SPECK IN THE COSMOS, ONCE WE REALIZE OUR CONNECTIONS
WITH EVERYTHING THAT IS, AND THAT THERE ARE NO LIMITS TO
OUR CONTRIBUTION, WE GAIN A SENSE OF SELF–WORTH AND PURPOSE.

1 Let your eyes rest on the centre of the mandala and its vibrant pentacle, a symbol of the wonder of life and of self-realization. Imagine that the power of its sacred geometry is flowing into you.

2 Look at the floating figure: this is one of us and all of us. It is you, and all the others with whom you share a bond of cosmic kinship. You are bestride the universe.

3 Next, transfer your attention to the flowers. Let the natural cycles they symbolize bathe you in purity (snowdrops), hope and renewal (daffodils), love (roses), self-truth (chrysanthemums) and protection (peonies).

4 Finally, let the stars at the periphery call your attention to the beautiful truth of creation. Each shining star is unique, despite being one of millions. So are you.

"The universe is transformation; our life is what our thoughts make it."

Marcus Aurelius (AD 121–180)

A FLOWER FOR ALL SEASONS

FLOWERS REMIND US OF THE BOUNTY OF NATURE AND THE PASSAGE OF TIME. THEY BLOSSOM AND FADE, AND THEIR VALUE IS NOT COMPROMISED BY THEIR IMPERMANENCE: IMAGINE HOW STALE, SPIRITUALLY SPEAKING, AN EVERLASTING FLOWER WOULD BE — LIKE A SYNTHETIC DECORATION, EXPEDIENT BUT UNWORTHY OF PRAISE. WE, TOO, BLOSSOM AND FADE, AND THE FLOWER ENCAPSULATES OUR DESTINY IN MINIATURE. WE PASS INTO ETERNITY, WHICH IS WITHOUT SUFFERING AND WITHOUT TRANSGRESSION. FIND A FLOWER ON WHICH TO MEDITATE — IDEALLY, ONE WITH OVERLAPPING PETALS WITHIN CONCENTRIC CIRCLES, LIKE A DAISY, A ROSE OR A CAMELLIA. THIS IS A NATURAL MANDALA. TAKE ITS GEOMETRY, ITS BEAUTY AND ITS SYMBOLISM DEEP INSIDE YOURSELF.

FLOWER POWER

"If we could see the miracle of a single flower clearly, our whole life would change."

The Buddha (*c.*563–*c.*483 BC)

SOUL FOOD

"Bread feeds the body, indeed, but flowers feed also the soul."

The Prophet Muhammad (569–632)

ETERNAL OM

OM IS THE SACRED SYLLABLE REPRESENTING THE SOUND THAT BROUGHT CREATION INTO BEING — THE DIVINE WORD. CREATIVE ENERGY IS THE SOURCE OF EVERYTHING. IN OUR OWN LIVES, IT UNDERLIES ALL OUR PERCEPTIONS. WE ARE NOT PASSIVE, WE ARE PROFOUNDLY ACTIVE.

1 Let your gaze settle on the golden OM (in Sanskrit) at the centre of this mandala. Let this symbol of creative force connect you with your own, ever-present creative energy.

2 Move your eyes outward to the Star of David, a meeting of two triangles. Their intertwining resembles the mixing within yourself of the mortal and the divine. Dwell here for a moment, aware of the connections.

3 Next, shift your gaze to the white birds within the points of the star. They stand for your freedom to express yourself, and the joy that this brings. Let yourself relax and experience a liberating sensation of flying.

4 Fly with the birds toward the flames — the fires of imagination and passion waiting to transform thoughts into action. Feel the pride of being true to your creative self.

"The possible's slow fuse is lit by the imagination."

Emily Dickinson (1830–1886)

FREEDOM IN FLIGHT

IT IS HARD TO IMAGINE LIFE WITHOUT BIRDS. THEIR SONG IS NATURE SINGING ITS OWN ANTHEM, AND THEIR FLIGHT IS A GLORIOUS REMINDER OF OUR OWN BEST ASPIRATIONS AND OF OUR DEEPEST SELF — FREE AND SOULFUL. BIRDS ALSO REPRESENT MESSAGES FROM THE DIVINE. THEY ARE MEDIATORS, MOVING FREELY BETWEEN PHYSICAL AND SPIRITUAL WORLDS, AS THE HUMAN MIND CAN WHEN IT SHAKES OFF ITS ATTACHMENTS AND CARES. IN THE *UPANISHADS*, TWO BIRDS IN THE COMIC TREE, ONE EATING AND ONE WATCHING, REPRESENT THE INDIVIDUAL AND THE UNIVERSAL SOUL. MEDITATE ON THIS IMAGE. VISUALIZE ALSO THE DOVE WITH THE OLIVE BRANCH HERALDING DRY LAND FOR NOAH AS THE FLOOD WATERS RECEDE. DRY LAND WOULD BE STERILE WITHOUT BIRDS.

LOOK SKYWARD

*"When thou seest an eagle,
thou seest a portion of genius; lift up thy head."*

William Blake (1757–1827)

DANCE, THEN FLY

*"It is no doubt possible to fly – but first you
must know how to dance like an angel."*

Friedrich Nietzsche (1844–1900)

MOONLIGHT EPIPHANY

IF WE LISTEN TO OUR INTUITION IT CAN LEAD US ALONG A HEALING PATH
THAT IS APPROPRIATE FOR EACH OF US RIGHT NOW. WE CAN EXPERIENCE
INTUITION AS FLASHES OF INSIGHT, VIVID DREAMS OR A SENSE OF DEEP
RECOGNITION. TUNE INTO AND TRUST THESE IRRATIONAL PERCEPTIONS.

1 Pass through the outer circle of the mandala, the rim of the moon – a gateway to the unconscious and the intuitive realm of profound understanding and truth.

2 Now bring your gaze inward, to the centre of the mandala, and to the river flowing smoothly around rocks. Go with the flow: imagine yourself dodging obstacles to your well-being with ease.

3 Notice the silvery fish, signs of wisdom, leaping from the water. Open yourself to the wise ideas jumping from your unconscious.

4 Move upstream toward the river's source, a well-spring of self-healing. Allow your eyes to be drawn toward the hills, subtly shaped like a sleeping woman, a sign of latent intuition. Even in sleep the moon and stars shine down, revealing where the wise self lies.

*"I have given you words of vision and wisdom ... Ponder them in
the silence of your soul, and then in freedom do your will."*

The Bhagavad Gita (*c*.5th century BC)

MOON MAGIC

As ancient peoples gazed at the changing moon, they wove stories about how, each month, the orb was devoured by animals or gods, then miraculously renewed. The moon's phases therefore gave rise to associations with the cycle of birth, life and death. Devise your own lunar healing ceremonies. Anchor your intentions for self-growth to the new and waxing moon, gaze at the full moon to recharge your energies, shed negative thoughts as the moon wanes. Think about the intertidal shore, which would not have existed were it not for moon-driven tides. This is where amphibious life began. We are all amphibious in having one foot in the flesh, one foot in the spirit.

REVELATION

"The moon abiding
In the midst of a tranquil mind;
Clouds break into light."

Dogen (1200–1253)

GATEWAY TO THE HEART

"The silver light, which, hallowing tree and tower,
Sheds beauty and deep softness o'er the whole,
Breathes also to the heart."

Lord Byron (1788–1824)

THE UNFOLDING NOW

THERE IS ONLY NOW — THOUGH, OF COURSE, THE MOMENT ELUDES US AS
SOON AS WE PAUSE TO NOTICE IT. IF WE CAN FULLY UNDERSTAND HOW
MOMENT BY MOMENT WE EXPERIENCE THE NOW, WHICH IS THE SAME NOW
EXPERIENCED BY TREES AND FLOWERS, WE GRASP A SUBSTANTIAL TRUTH.

1 Bring your gaze to the cross of silhouetted figures. Feel the vibrant energy streaming toward you from the coloured chakra centres on the four bodies. Breathe in the power and potential of this unfolding moment.

2 Follow the coloured chakras to the crown of each head. They are so balanced and in tune with now that serpentine energy spills over from one moment into the next.

3 Now find the outstretched arms embracing each moment and stretching out to the trees. Imagine your awareness and senses opening right now like buds so that you can draw in the oaks' strength and the acorns' potential.

4 Finally, let your gaze settle on the point at which the human and tree trunks merge, grounded in the moment. Absorbing strength and balance, simply be here, now.

"Now. This is it. The whole purpose and meaning for the existence of everything."

Zen saying

HEALING MOTION

WHEN YOU EMBRACE RATHER THAN RESIST CHANGE, YOU BEGIN TO LIVE
WITH A FLUIDITY THAT FREES UP ENERGY FOR HEALTHY LIVING. THIS
MANDALA, INCORPORATING TRIGRAMS (AS PRESENTED IN THE *I CHING*),
CARRIES YOU INTO THE FUTURE ON STREAMS OF EVER-CHANGING ENERGY.

1 Start with your gaze at the centre
of the mandala, where the wheel of
the year emerges from a spiral of light.
Sense time unrolling around you,
moment after moment, bringing with it
the potential for change.

2 Let your eyes rest on the elements
you need to grasp to ground yourself in
changing creation: solid earth, the air of
the higher realms, inner fire and ever-
flowing water.

3 Now look at the three-line trigrams
against their turquoise background.
See how their varying short and longer
lines ring the changes on a world of
potential. Allow the possibilities they
symbolize to permeate deep into your
being.

4 Picture the eight-pointed star
bursting forth, a dynamo of power
whose structure holds ever firm while
it pulses out light.

*"They must often change, who would be
constant in happiness or wisdom."*

Confucius (551–479 BC)

EVER MOVING FORWARD

*"Keeping adding, keep walking,
keep advancing."*

St Augustine (354–430)

UNIVERSAL TRUTH

"All things change; nothing perishes."

Ovid (43 BC–AD 17)

CASTING CHANGES

THE *I CHING*, OR *BOOK OF CHANGES*, IS A CLASSICAL CHINESE TEXT MADE UP OF A SYSTEM OF SYMBOLS USED TO MAKE PREDICTIONS AND OFFER ADVICE. IT IS BASED ON THE EIGHT TRIGRAM SYMBOLS SHOWN IN THE MANDALA ON PAGE 197. EACH IS AN ARRANGEMENT OF SOLID (YANG) AND BROKEN (YIN) LINES. SYMBOLIZED IN THIS IS THE TAOIST BELIEF THAT THE COSMOS IS BASED ON A CONSTANT FLUX OF COMPLEMENTARY FORCES. THE TRIGRAMS ARE COMBINED TO FORM 64 POSSIBLE HEXAGRAMS. TO CAST THE I CHING, YOU THROW YARROW STICKS — LIKE THROWING DICE. CHANCE, IT IS IMPLIED, IS NEVER RANDOM: IT ALIGNS ITSELF TO THE GRAIN OF OUR DESTINY. THIS DOES NOT IMPEDE FREE WILL, BUT SIMPLY MEANS THAT NO EVENT IS WITHOUT SIGNIFICANCE.

JEWEL IN THE LOTUS

IN EASTERN TRADITIONS, THE LOTUS IS A SYMBOL OF THE UNSULLIED HEART OR SOUL, RISING FROM THE MUDDY WATERS OF HUMAN IMPERFECTIONS. OUR INNER BEAUTY, ONCE WE NOURISH IT, BLOSSOMS TO REVEAL ASTONISHING PURITY, LIKE THE LOTUS OPENING TO THE SUN.

1 Rest your eyes on the luminous diamond unfolded by the lotus. It represents the value of your hidden depths and an invincible strength born from pressure.

2 Now contemplate the petals themselves. They show the beauty of your generous soul, a flowering of love – strength, giving, compassion and beauty fused.

3 Shift your gaze to the rising sun behind the diamond and lotus – the eternal divine that inspires the divine in ourselves to emerge.

4 Finally, find the halo of pearls – wisdom through experience. Let their gentle sheen be a reflection of the inner beauty shining out from you. They give you self-esteem and a protective outer ring of many virtues.

"Though we travel the world over to find the beautiful,
we must carry it with us, or we find it not."

Ralph Waldo Emerson (1803–1882)

LOOK WITHIN

"Many individuals have, like uncut diamonds,
shining qualities beneath a rough exterior."

Juvenal (late 1st/early 2nd century AD)

SMOOTHING THE SOUL

"The soul is placed in the body like a rough diamond,
and must be polished, or the lustre of it will never appear."

Daniel Defoe (1660–1731)

ENDURING BRILLIANCE

DIAMONDS HAVE BEEN REVERED SINCE ANTIQUITY. THE ANCIENT GREEKS BELIEVED THAT THEY WERE THE TEARS OF THE GODS, WHILE THE ROMANS CONSIDERED THEM TO BE FRAGMENTS OF FALLING STARS. THE EXTRAORDINARY PHYSICAL PROPERTIES OF THE DIAMOND — THE WORLD'S HARDEST MATERIAL — MAKE IT AN APT SYMBOL OF ENDURING LOVE, PURITY, STRENGTH, COURAGE AND INDESTRUCTIBILITY. WITHIN EASTERN SPIRITUAL TEACHINGS, THIS GEMSTONE IS ALSO USED AS AN ANALOGY OF THE SOUL, WHICH ENDURES THROUGH COUNTLESS INCARNATIONS WITH ITS PURITY OF INTENTION UNTARNISHED. DIAMONDS ARE SAID TO OPEN A PORTAL TO SPIRITUAL GROWTH. SIT QUIETLY AND MEDITATE ON THE QUALITIES OF A DIAMOND.

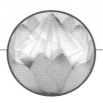

RIPPLING WATERS

WATER CAN SOOTHE THE MIND: GAZING AT THE VASTNESS OF THE OCEAN
PUTS WORRIES INTO PERSPECTIVE, WHILE LOOKING INTO A STILL LAKE
OR POND CAN GUIDE US INTO A RELAXED STATE IN WHICH WE CAN
EXPERIENCE TRUE INSIGHT AND SHED ILLUSIONS WITHOUT PANIC.

1 Look into the centre of the mandala, at the flower-head floating on the surface of a deep pool. Imagine you yourself are floating, in air rather than in water, as you look down into the depths. You feel safe and relaxed.

2 Now gaze into the pool as it ripples in circles. A wind is stirring its surface, but down below lies deep calm. Let its tranquillity permeate deep inside you.

3 Now bring your attention to the willow leaves overhanging the pool's edges. They are firmly connected to the bank, yet flourish in the air. Your inner stillness shares their grounded flexibility.

4 Lastly, take in the mandala as a whole, with its border of pebbles and flowers and its lily-pad corners. Feel its ripples spread through your mind in an endless flow.

"If water derives clarity from stillness, how much more so does the mind!"

Zhuangzi (c.369–286 BC)

Wild-Horse Winds

THE HORSE IS A FASCINATING ANIMAL — STRANGELY HUMAN IN ITS INTELLIGENCE YET TOTALLY OTHER IN ITS FOUR-LEGGED FORM. HERE, WE CONNECT WITH ITS HEALING FORCE, MAGNIFIED BY THE WINDS OF CHANGE. LEAP WITH THESE HORSES TO FREEDOM AND WELL-BEING.

1 Find the vortex of energy at the mandala's centre, where a wind is rising. Watch it spin a spiral of leaves and let this blow away your anxieties. The brown leaves signify all you have outgrown, and green is for regeneration.

2 Now gaze at the galloping horses, feeling your energy increase, and past fears fall away. Embrace the horses' freedom. Trust them: they in turn will trust you and your kindness.

3 Expand your awareness to the ring of laurel leaves, traditionally used to crown a great poet. In so doing, you discover the poetry of your own spirit.

4 Finally, look at the grounding shape of interlocking squares, and the broken chains in its corners. Mentally sever your connection with everything that holds you back and enjoy the healing sense of release this brings.

"When you ... are unable to control your mind, your senses do not obey you, just as unruly horses do not obey a charioteer."

Upanishads (*c.*1000 BC)

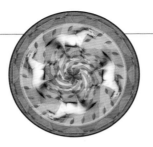

THE WINDS OF CHANGE

BEING OUTSIDE ON A WINDY DAY IS EXHILARATING. WE FEEL THE ENERGY OF NATURE, AND IT CAN SEEM AS IF OUR COBWEBS OF ANXIETY, DEPRESSION OR TIREDNESS ARE BEING BLOWN AWAY BY A FORCE THAT FINDS THEM IRRELEVANT — A FORCE SEEN AND HEARD, YET INVISIBLE IN ITSELF. WIND IS COUSIN TO AIR AND TO BREATH, HENCE THE IMPORTANCE OF ITS SYMBOLISM. IT CLEARS US OF CLUTTER, LIFTS OUR SPIRITS AND REARRANGES THE FAMILIAR. A SAILING SHIP WITHOUT WIND WOULD BE AS USELESS AS A BODY WITHOUT A SOUL, OR A HUMAN BEING WITHOUT A CLEAR SENSE OF THEIR OWN DESTINY. OUR WIND CHIMES, WHICH TELL US THAT LIFE IS CHANGE, ARE ALL AROUND US: LISTEN TO THE RUSTLING OF LEAVES WHENEVER YOU CAN, FOR THERE WAS NEVER A TRUER WORD SPOKEN.

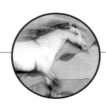

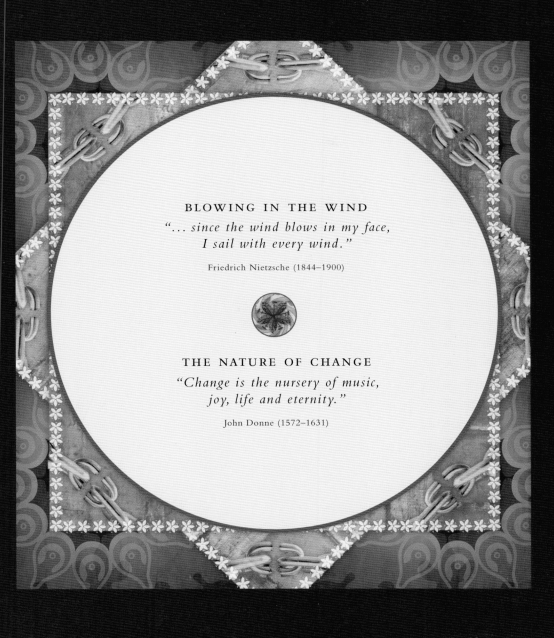

BLOWING IN THE WIND

"... since the wind blows in my face,
I sail with every wind."

Friedrich Nietzsche (1844–1900)

THE NATURE OF CHANGE

"Change is the nursery of music,
joy, life and eternity."

John Donne (1572–1631)

TRIPLE SPIRAL

THE INTERLOCKING CURLICUES OF A TRIPLE SPIRAL SHOW THE WHOLENESS OF MIND, SPIRIT AND MATTER. IN THE UNION OF THE TRINITY, THE MEETING OF EARTH, WATER AND SKY, THE INTERTWINING OF PAST, PRESENT AND FUTURE, WE FIND MODELS FOR THE INTEGRATED SELF.

1 Let your gaze rest on the entire mandala. Relax into the unity and completeness of all its elements. If you feel a sense of movement within the mandala, go with it. Feel how balance and movement co-exist.

2 Now focus on the large triple spiral and its central point, which represents your concentrated essence. Let your eyes trace the three distinct coils – mind, body and spirit. Recall the spiral progress of your learning, spreading out from well-earned knowledge.

3 Move your gaze out to the beads threaded around the triple spiral. Each is separate and perfect, yet interconnects with the others to create a circle of beauty and harmony.

4 Finally, find the four shells in the corners. Even nature echoes the integrated self.

"The gate of the soul will be flung wide open once complete harmony of the body, mind and spirit is attained."

Indian proverb

RAINBOW UNION

EACH OF US HAS A DUAL NATURE: MASCULINE AND FEMININE, ACTIVE AND
RECEPTIVE, LOGICAL AND INTUITIVE. BALANCING THESE SEEMINGLY POLAR
ENERGIES WITHIN OURSELVES IS A HEALING EXPERIENCE THAT EQUIPS US
TO MEET A LIFE PARTNER WHOSE QUALITIES COMPLEMENT OURS.

1 Pour your gaze into the golden chalice, vessel of your feminine qualities. Now focus on the sword of determination, symbol of your masculine energy. Sense these opposites move toward each other at the centre of the mandala – reflecting their potential to come together within yourself and your relationship.

2 Now look at the interlinked male/female signs. They represent your true, dual nature. Feel intuition and reason merging in a union you can both celebrate.

3 Trace the repeating "lemniscates" – the figures of eight that reach out to connect the linked male and female signs in perfect harmony.

4 Finally, seek out the rainbows, whose colours echo those of your chakras. They bless the union of opposites.

"I am a part of all that I have met."

Alfred, Lord Tennyson (1809–1892)

LANGUAGE OF COLOUR

"Mere colour, unspoiled by meaning and unallied with definite form, can speak to the soul in a thousand different ways."

Oscar Wilde (1854–1900)

BE THOU THE RAINBOW

"Be thou the rainbow in the storms of life. The evening beam that smiles the clouds away, and tints tomorrow with prophetic ray."

Lord Byron (1788–1824)

A HEALING SPECTRUM

THE MYSTICAL BEAUTY OF A RAINBOW COMES FROM THE PRISM CREATED BY DROPLETS OF WATER IN THE AIR FOLLOWING RAIN. ITS HARMONIOUS COLOURS REMIND US THAT WHEN LIFE'S STORMS PASS, THERE CAN, ONCE AGAIN, BE PEACE IF WE BELIEVE IN IT AND LOOK FOR IT. THE RAINBOW IS A UNIVERSAL SYMBOL OF INTERDEPENDENCY, AS WELL AS A BRIDGE BETWEEN THE EARTHLY REALM AND THE UNSEEN. IN THE BODY, ITS SEVEN COLOURS ARE ASSOCIATED WITH THE MAJOR CHAKRAS, FROM RED AT THE BASE TO VIOLET AT THE CROWN. WHEN YOU SEE A RAINBOW, LET IT REMIND YOU TO LOOK FOR THE BEAUTY OF THE SOUL WITHIN. BUT THINK TOO OF THE "RAINBOW NATION" — THE IDEAL OF A PEACEFUL MIXED SOCIETY THAT DEPENDS ON ENLIGHTENED PEOPLE PASSING ON THEIR WISDOM.

HEALING MIRROR

TWO HANDS THAT COME TOGETHER IN A GESTURE OF PRAYER FOR OTHERS
CAN CHANGE THE WORLD — BY REJECTING SELFISHNESS AND SPREADING
COMPASSION. THESE ARE HANDS THAT COULD BE BUSY IN ACQUISITIVE
ACTIVITY, BUT INSTEAD THEY STOP AND PERFORM A SELFLESS CEREMONY.

1 Rest your gaze on the yin–yang symbol in the centre of the mandala. See how each half envelops an element of the other. Appreciate the dynamic union of the pairing.

2 Now shift your attention to the pairs of reflected hands. See how, in their perfect mirror image, they denote not the vanity we often associate with mirrors, but selfless prayer. The cross these pairs of hands form symbolizes the perfect interfusion of humanity and divinity.

3 Widen your focus to take in the humming birds sipping from flowers — such is the succour given if we honour each other.

4 Finally, take in the perfectly reflected image in its entirety. Feel yourself effortlessly relaxing into a state of healing symmetry.

"The heart of man is made to reconcile the most glaring contradictions."

David Hume (1711–1776)

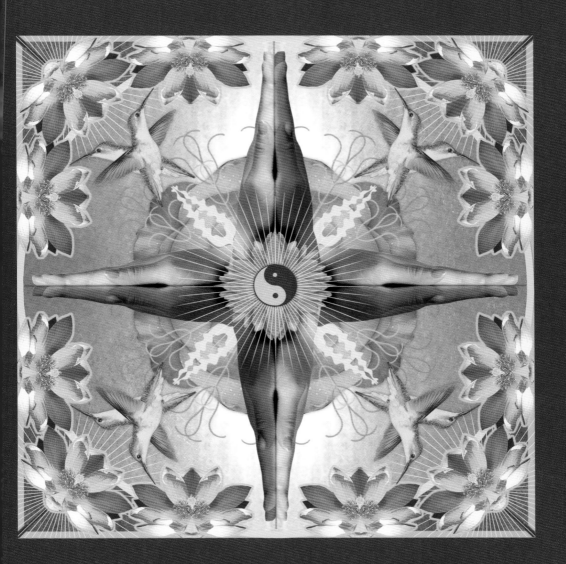

UNITY WITHIN

TWO TREES SHARING ONE ROOT SYSTEM ARE A POTENT EXPRESSION OF
INDEPENDENCE COMBINED WITH DEPENDENCE. THIS MANDALA USES
SUCH SYMBOLISM TO SHOW THE STRENGTH OF A HEALTHY RELATIONSHIP,
MARRED BY NEITHER SERVILE WEAKNESS NOR OVERBEARING STRENGTH.

1 Take in the solid separateness of
the twin tree trunks. Then turn to
their canopy of leaves mingling
in the air and their roots merging
underground. Beyond the duality
of individuals lies peaceful unity.

2 Contemplate the balances within
the mandala: earth and air, yin and
yang, light and shade. This mirrors the
perfect meeting of body and mind and
the pure connection – physical, mental

and spiritual – between two people.
Register this symbol, with its opposites,
and let it rest in your consciousness.

3 Focus on the contrasting cranes.
Imagine them crossing paths,
exchanging positions and colours
as they move through shadow and
sunlight. Magical transformations
take place when two people unite
in harmony.

"Grow in each other's shade, and share the rain."

Mareo Aleman (1547–*c.*1609)

A DOME OVER ALL

THE IMAGE OF THE DOME, AS FOUND IN MANY PLACES OF WORSHIP
OF DIFFERENT FAITHS, REPRESENTS THE COSMOS BUT ALSO, LESS
PRECISELY, THE POSSIBILITY OF INTER-FAITH HARMONY IF ONLY
SECTARIAN AND POLITICAL DIFFERENCES COULD BE HEALED.

1 Let your gaze rest on the eye in the centre of the mandala. Your wise self, this eye sits here as the "I" who witnesses and understands all without passing judgment.

2 Redirect your eyes to the frame through which this eye gazes – it looks out on four shining temples, each with its own dome. The mandala as a whole also represents a dome, seen in plan, with the heavens above.

3 Shift your gaze to the starry cosmos, in which no distinction of doctrine carries significance. Contrasting with the night, the golden dome shows the beauty that humankind can achieve, within themselves, when inspired by spirit rather than prejudice.

4 Finally, meditate on the eight soaring birds, symbolizing freedom of worship and proximity to the divine.

"Life, like a dome of many-coloured glass,
Stains the white radiance of Eternity."

Percy Bysshe Shelley (1792–1822)

THE PILLARS OF TRUTH

"Every truth has four corners. As a teacher
I give you one corner, and it is for you to find
the other three."

Confucius (551–479 BC)

REVEALED KNOWLEDGE

"Jesus said: 'What is hidden from you will be
disclosed to you. ... Split a piece of wood, I am there.
Raise the stone, and you will find me there.'"

The Gospel of St Thomas (c.50–140)

SACRED TEACHERS

As a privileged minority today in the West, we have the freedom to choose our own faith by accepting or rejecting certain doctrines. Hence we may come to believe in the One, the "power of now", loving-kindness — and indeed mandala meditation. However, we should never forget that the greatest thoughts humankind has had, about the spirit and enlightenment, have come from individuals — wise ones who have inspired not only by their words but also by their deeds. If you happen to come across a good teacher, think yourself lucky and take every opportunity to learn. Otherwise, read widely, think deeply and remember that your latest thoughts are not necessarily your wisest.

WINGS OF PEACE

THE BIBLICAL IMAGE OF THE DOVE CARRYING THE OLIVE BRANCH
SUGGESTS NOT ONLY HOPE BUT ALSO RECONCILIATION — GOD MAKING
PEACE WITH THE WORLD. THIS MANDALA DEPLOYS BOTH SYMBOLS TO
BRING PEACE INTO THE HEART OF THE MEDITATOR.

1 Gaze at the flower unfolding in the centre of the mandala. Feel yourself relaxing into it. Sense yourself gradually blossoming into your natural state of peace — all enmity has withered away.

2 Fly with this peace on the wings of the doves. Lovely flowers bloom in peace's shadow. Imagine spreading loving wings around all who have hurt you.

3 Flying out into the world, you reach a circle of olive leaves. These are the hope that your peace will pacify others — it will if you believe it will.

4 Finally, gaze at the outer circle with its tiny flower-heads. Loving relationships with all, based on peace and forgiveness, nurture beauty in unexpected places. Be a gardener of love and beauty in the soil of peace.

"First keep the peace within yourself, then you can also bring peace to others."

Thomas à Kempis (1380–1471)

AFTER THE FLOOD

"And the dove came in to him in the evening; and, lo, in her mouth was an olive leaf pluckt off: so Noah knew that the waters were abated from off the earth."

Genesis 8.11

GENTLY, GENTLY

"Thoughts that come with doves' footsteps guide the world."

Friedrich Nietzsche (1844–1900)

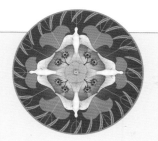

THE DOVE RETURNS

In the biblical story of the Flood, Noah released first a raven and then a dove to search for land. When the dove returned bearing an olive branch in its bill, this marked a new epoch after a time of loss and hardship, and so the bird came to stand as a symbol of peace and hope. The dove's universal associations with peace owe nothing to its nature — it is often quarrelsome — and much to its pure white beauty. Another important meaning attached to doves is the Holy Spirit: when John the Baptist baptized Christ, he saw the Spirit of God descending upon him "like a dove". By meditating on the dove, we access the possibility of perceiving divinity in our hearts.

MYSTIC RINGS

LOVE, WHICH COMES FROM OUR UNADULTERATED SPIRIT,
HAS THE CAPACITY TO BE ETERNAL AND PURE. WE SPEAK OF "FOR EVER"
WITH NO THOUGHT OF MORTALITY, BECAUSE MORTALITY SPEAKS
A LANGUAGE FOREIGN TO THE PURE OF HEART.

1 Focus on the pink shell in the centre of the mandala. Let its colour pour unconditional love into your heart. Let its spiral shape remind you that love is natural and beautiful.

2 Broaden your gaze out to the interlinked rings that form a *vesica piscis*, a sign of the sacred marriage of matter and spirit. Make a solemn promise to yourself that you will live in the spirit of this union.

3 Now follow the energy of love as its rays stream out from the Earth to honour the sun and moon. You have joined in a cosmic community of love. Remember the ending of Dante's *Il Paradiso*: "The love that moves the sun and other stars."

4 Finally, be enveloped in love's angelic wings as you glide effortlessly to the rim of the mandala. You are poised to fly free.

"… the moments when you have truly lived are the moments
when you have done things in the spirit of love."

Henry Drummond (1851–1897)

LIKE A BUTTERFLY

IN HEALTHY RELATIONSHIPS, WE OFFER OTHERS HELP AND SUPPORT
TO DEVELOP THEIR POTENTIAL, ALLOWING THEM TO SPREAD THEIR
WINGS AND BECOME MORE FULLY THEMSELVES. THIS CAN TAKE COURAGE
AND ENERGY, BUT TRANSFORMS BOTH GIVER AND RECEIVER.

1 Focus on the caterpillars and cocoons or chrysalises in the centre of the mandala. The butterfly growing inside each one expends its energy to break out and spread its wings. Relationships, too, need effort and energy.

2 Beyond, find the diamond-shaped space where a relationship can grow. Sense the adult butterflies' antennae alert to every movement. Alertness to another is a sign of love.

3 Next, shift your gaze to the four butterflies. They will take off in turn to find their destiny – first the upper two, then the two beneath, in an orderly dance of love.

4 Finally, focus on the suns and the moons in the circular rim of the mandala. A moon covers each sun, although without eclipsing it. The sun's rays blaze out undimmed. You feel at rest and in harmony.

*"Happiness is like a butterfly which, when pursued, is ... beyond
our grasp, but if you will sit down quietly, may alight upon you."*

Nathaniel Hawthorne (1804–1864)

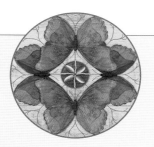

A CELESTIAL PAIRING

THE SUN AND MOON EXIST ON TOTALLY DIFFERENT SCALES OF MAGNITUDE AND DISTANCE — THE SUN IS A FIERY GIANT IN ANOTHER REALM, THE MOON OUR DIMINUTIVE NEIGHBOUR. THE DIFFERENCE BETWEEN A SUN AND A SATELLITE IS VAST. IF IN TERMS OF SYMBOLISM THEY HAVE A CLOSER KINSHIP, THIS IS BECAUSE OUR VIEWPOINT SEES THEM AS HEAVENLY BODIES THAT RISE AND SET, WITHIN THE CYCLE OF DAY AND NIGHT. THIS NEAR-SIGHTED TRUTH IS VALID, YET THERE IS A FAR-SIGHTED WISDOM BEYOND IT: THE SHEER IMMENSITY OF CREATION, THE WONDER OF ITS UNCONQUERABLE SPACES, AND THE HUMAN SPIRIT IN THE MIDST OF IT ALL — HUMBLE, ETERNAL, PROUD AND NO LESS BEAUTIFUL THAN THE SUN OR MOON.

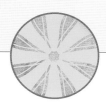

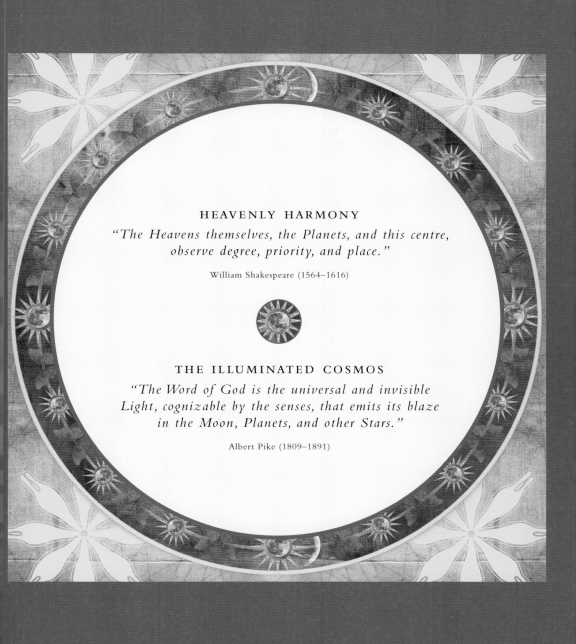

HEAVENLY HARMONY

*"The Heavens themselves, the Planets, and this centre,
observe degree, priority, and place."*

William Shakespeare (1564–1616)

THE ILLUMINATED COSMOS

*"The Word of God is the universal and invisible
Light, cognizable by the senses, that emits its blaze
in the Moon, Planets, and other Stars."*

Albert Pike (1809–1891)

LADY OF COMPASSION

COMPASSION IS PERSONALIZED HERE AS THE GODDESS OF COMPASSION,
WHO DELAYED HER OWN SALVATION UNTIL SHE HAD SAVED ALL SOULS ON
EARTH. SHE IS DEPICTED IN A MEDITATION POSE, SENDING HER LOVING-
KINDNESS OUTWARD FROM A HEART FULL OF LOVE.

1 Focus on the Goddess of Compassion in the centre of the mandala. Open your heart to her unconditional love and acceptance. Feel confident that her endless compassion is pouring out to you, enabling you to be compassionate in turn.

2 Now rest in the ring of soft, heart-shaped petals. Feel the blooming of compassion inside yourself, like a warm glow.

3 Let your eyes drift to the little circles containing miniature deities. The Goddess of Compassion's tiny form can nestle inside every human heart, including yours. Think of the goddess in every atom of every in-breath and out-breath.

4 Take your gaze to the mandala's surround, the lovely flowers that bloom when compassion's seeds fall on fertile soil.

*"Our sorrows and wounds are healed only
when we touch them with compassion."*

The Buddha (c.563–c.483 BC)

THE MERCIFUL GODDESS

THE GODDESS OF COMPASSION HAS BEEN VENERATED IN MANY CULTURES UNDER DIFFERENT GUISES — FROM ANCIENT EGYPT'S ISIS TO CHINA'S KUAN YIN. IN TIBET, SHE IS KNOWN AS TARA, THE FEMININE ASPECT OF THE BUDDHA, WHO AS A BODHISATTVA, OR ENLIGHTENED BEING, CHOOSES TO FORGO THE PERMANENT BLISS OF NIRVANA IN ORDER TO HELP OTHERS. HER ANCESTOR IS THE MALE BODHISATTVA, AVALOKITESHVARA. SHE EMBODIES UNCONDITIONAL LOVE, ACCEPTANCE, MERCY AND FORGIVENESS, AND IS OFTEN APPEALED TO IN TIMES OF DISTRESS FOR PROTECTION, COMFORT AND HEALING — SHE IS KNOWN IN ALL CULTURES AS "SHE WHO LISTENS TO THE CRIES OF THE WORLD". IN ONE LEGEND, SHE IS GRANTED A THOUSAND ARMS TO HELP HER IN HER ENDLESS ALMSGIVING.

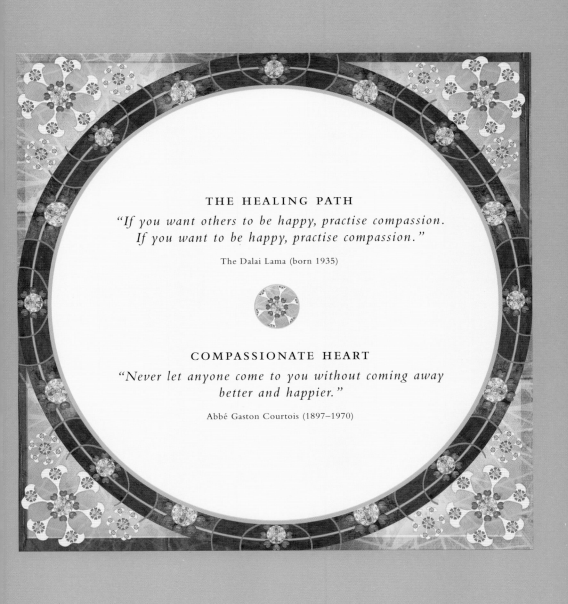

THE HEALING PATH

*"If you want others to be happy, practise compassion.
If you want to be happy, practise compassion."*

The Dalai Lama (born 1935)

COMPASSIONATE HEART

*"Never let anyone come to you without coming away
better and happier."*

Abbé Gaston Courtois (1897–1970)

A CUP OVERFLOWING

THE CUP OF PLENTY FREELY BESTOWS NOURISHMENT IN WHATEVER FORM
IS REQUIRED. IN THIS MANDALA MEDITATION, IT POURS FORGIVENESS —
THE MOST EFFECTIVE BALM FOR HEALING THE HEART. BUT YOU MAY ADAPT
THE MEDITATION TO LOVE, OR PEACE, OR WISDOM IF YOU WISH.

1 Start by contemplating the spiral *bindu* at the very centre of the mandala – this is your self, saturated with the potential for forgiveness, and about to set off on the inner journey that will win it as your treasure.

2 Look at the centrally placed golden chalice, its water spilling abundantly onto the earth. Think of this as forgiveness in endless supply.

3 Meditate on the perfect pattern of reconciliation made by the flowing waters. Forgiveness forms around the pattern in your heart – a geometry of love and peace.

4 Travel out from the circle of potentiality – the round table on which the chalice stands. The first flowing circle is forgiveness in your heart. Move to the outer flowing circle – a commitment to enacting forgiveness.

"In giving, a man receives more than he gives,
and the more is in proportion to the worth of the thing given."

George MacDonald (1824–1905)

THE CHALICE

IN IRISH LEGEND, WE ENCOUNTER THE CHALICE AS THE CAULDRON OF DAGDA, WHICH GRANTS THE WISHES OF ALL WHO COME INTO ITS PRESENCE. LATER, AS THE HOLY GRAIL, A CHALICE BECOMES A CENTRAL FOCUS IN THE ARTHURIAN LEGEND, BEING AVAILABLE ONLY TO THOSE WHO ARE WORTHY AND WHO PASS RIGOROUS TESTS. IN CHRISTIANITY, THE TEST IS A CALL TO FAITH: THE GRAIL WAS THOUGHT TO BE THE CUP FROM WHICH CHRIST DRANK AT THE LAST SUPPER OR IN WHICH BLOOD WAS GATHERED FROM HIS SIDE DURING THE CRUCIFIXION. TO INTEGRATE THE SYMBOLIC CHALICE INTO YOUR OWN LIFE, CONSIDER YOUR SOUL AS A VESSEL: VALUABLE FOR WHAT IT CONTAINS, AND CARRYING OUT ITS PROPER PURPOSE ONLY WHEN FULL TO THE BRIM AND BEYOND, NOT WHEN SITTING EMPTY AS A TROPHY.

KARMIC RECKONING

*"A human act once set in motion
flows on for ever to the great account."*

George Meredith (1828–1909)

OUR HOLY GRAIL

*"For one human being to love another: that is perhaps
the most difficult of our tasks; the ultimate,
the last test and proof, the work for which
all other work is but preparation."*

Rainer Maria Rilke (1875–1926)

ANOTHER'S FIRE

ONCE THE SPIRIT INSIDE YOU IS IGNITED BY A TRUE SENSE OF YOUR
WORTH, IT BURNS AWAY THE DROSS TO ALLOW YOUR ESSENTIAL NATURE
TO SHINE THROUGH. THIS MANDALA MOVES OUTSIDE THE SELF AND ASKS
YOU TO INHABIT, SYMBOLICALLY, THE SPIRIT OF SOMEONE ELSE.

1 Start with the pearl at the centre of
the mandala – the spirit of your friend,
in concentrated essence. All his or her
thoughts, actions and emotions proceed
from this pearl, fostered within the
oyster of inheritance and experience.

2 See the flames of action radiate from
this person as they move through life,
connecting powerfully with those
around them.

3 Observe how the blazing pearl of this
person is at the centre of their own web
of life. You yourself are a shining thread
in this web – strong, connected and one
of many.

4 Broaden your focus to take in the
entire mandala – a beautiful outpouring
of energy, constantly in motion yet
always forming a perfect pattern around
its centre. Send loving thoughts to feed
your friend's flames.

"The most powerful weapon on earth is the human soul on fire."

Ferdinand Foch (1851–1929)

THE WEB OF LIFE

WE ARE ALL PART OF A COMPLEX WEB OF LIFE. EVERY SPECIES ON OUR PLANET, FROM THE TINIEST ORGANISM TO THE LARGEST MAMMAL, CONTRIBUTES TO THE HEALTH AND BALANCE OF THE WHOLE. WE MIGHT COMPARE THIS TO A SPIDER'S WEB, IN WHICH THE SLIGHTEST MOVEMENT SENDS VIBRATIONS THROUGH THE ENTIRE SUBTLE YET RESILIENT STRUCTURE. OFTEN, WE FEEL THE NEED FOR HEALING BECAUSE WE HAVE LOST OUR CONNECTION WITH OTHER PARTS OF THIS WEB — FAMILY, FRIENDS, A SPIRITUAL COMMUNITY. BEGIN TO REDISCOVER THE ENERGIES OF THE WEB BY STRENGTHENING BONDS WITH LOVED ONES. AS YOU DO SO, WATCH HOW LOVE AND COMPASSION FORTIFY YOUR INNER LIFE AND SPREAD OUT INTO THE WORLD, ATTRACTING KINDRED SPIRITS TO RECONNECT YOU TO THE WHOLE.

MILLIONS TAKE PART

*"In the entire universe there are myriad forms
and millions of blades of grass, and each ...
are, one by one, the entire universe."*

Dogen (1200–1253)

LINKS IN THE CHAIN OF BEING

*"Earthworms, though in appearance a small and
despicable link in the chain of nature, yet, if lost,
would make a lamentable chasm."*

Gilbert White (1720–1793)

Spiral River

WATER TAKES THE PATH OF LEAST RESISTANCE, FLOWING WITH
EASE AROUND OBSTACLES. MEDITATING ON A RIVER, THEREFORE, HELPS
THE MIND TO STAY FLUID IN TROUBLED TIMES. INSTEAD OF FIGHTING THE
CURRENT, ALLOW THE RIVER'S ENERGY TO CARRY YOU TO NEW SHORES.

1 Rest your gaze on the central yin-yang symbol, sign of duality: the complementary opposites of life. Then follow the spiral flow of the water – a magic river without turbulence, which flows inside us all.

2 Take in the scenery as you float past the river banks: grasses give way to trees, which give way to rocks. All are unaffected by your problems, and so, in truth, are you.

3 Feel the persistent flow deepening the river by constant erosion of the river bed. Our resilience in the face of problems deepens us similarly: there is no difficulty life can throw at us that doesn't enable us to grow.

4 At the end of your spiral voyage, once you have weathered the immediate crisis, find yourself in a space of endless possibility. Your life is as rich as you choose.

*"Water is fluid, soft and yielding. But water will wear away rock,
which is rigid and cannot yield ... what is soft is strong."*

Tao Te Ching (6th century BC)

SPIRAL ENERGY

THE SPIRAL IS A COMMON SHAPE IN NATURE, FOUND IN THE COMPLEX DOUBLE-HELIX STRUCTURE OF DNA, IN SHELLS, COILED SERPENTS, WHIRLPOOLS AND GALAXIES. WHEN OUR DISTANT ANCESTORS BEGAN TO MAKE ART, THE SHAPE WAS ENGRAVED INTO ROCKS AND DRAWN ON CAVE WALLS. THIS SYMBOLIC SPIRAL IS RICH IN MEANING. IT HAS COME TO REPRESENT EVOLUTION, THE CYCLES OF THE SEASONS AND OF LIFE, SELF-TRANSFORMATION, AND THE DEVELOPMENT OF UNDERSTANDING, KNOWLEDGE AND WISDOM. IT ALSO HAS LINKS WITH FEMININE POWER AND FERTILITY (THE INWARD SPIRAL) AND WITH MASCULINE ENERGY (THE UNCOILING SPIRAL). THE CONTINUOUS CONCENTRIC AND PROGRESSIVE MOTION OF THE SPIRAL SUGGESTS THE VERY RHYTHM OF LIFE ITSELF.

SPIRAL RHYTHMS

"Progress has not followed a straight ascending line,
but a spiral with rhythms of progress and retrogression,
of evolution and dissolution."

Johann Wolfgang von Goethe (1749–1832)

A LIFE OF CHANGE

"Nothing is secure but life, transition,
the energizing spirit."

Ralph Waldo Emerson (1803–1882)

FLOATING CLOUDS

FEAR IS A NATURAL DEFENCE IN TIMES OF DANGER, BUT ALL TOO OFTEN OUR FEARS ARE BASED ON IMAGINED PERILS. FAR BEYOND ITS CAUSE, FEAR CAN GROW AND TAKE US OVER LIKE AN ALIEN LIFE-FORM. THIS MANDALA ENCOURAGES YOU TO LET GO OF FEARS TO REVEAL YOUR TRUE SELF.

1 Rest your gaze on the clouds within the mandala – fears that drift over the sky of consciousness. See how wispy they are: they fail to blot out the force of the sun – the strong centre of the mandala and of your being.

2 Now turn your attention to the sun as it sets over the still water. Feel its gentle warmth melting away the clouds moment by moment, and watch them losing even what strength they had. In the coming darkness, these clouds pose no threat.

3 Find the butterflies and birds on the rim of the mandala – the flight from fear is a journey toward wholeness.

4 Finally, bathe in the mandala as in a fortifying pool, breathing in its golden energy and its reflective peace.

"The mind should be a vastness like the sky.
Mental events should be allowed to disperse like clouds."

Longchenpa (1308–1363)

TEARDROP HEALING

WHETHER WE HAVE LOST A FRIEND, A LOVED ONE, A JOB OR A
LONG-HELD DREAM, GRIEVING IS A HEALING PROCESS THAT ENABLES
US TO WORK THROUGH THE PROGRESS OF NATURAL EMOTIONS TO ARRIVE
IN THE END AT ACCEPTANCE AND RESTORED PEACE.

1 Start at the dark centre of the mandala. Simply sit here with your feelings and halt the temptation to push grief away. Instead, give yourself space to simply feel.

2 Move your focus to the four streams of tears, recognizing their cooling, cleansing potential. See each tear as a healing drop of rain. Give yourself permission to let tears flow if you feel it will help.

3 Follow the tears, drop by drop, from the dark inner circle to the pale green outer circle – the zone of recovery. You may not feel ready to enter the outer zone wholeheartedly yet, but you will in time.

4 Gaze at the fresh growth springing from soil watered by tears – the shoots and full-blown flowers. These may represent wisdom now, but later they may suggest renewal.

"One's suffering disappears when one lets oneself go,
when one yields – even to sadness."

Antoine de Saint-Exupéry (1900–1944)

PURIFYING THE SOUL

"Wash away, Waters, whatever sin is in me, what wrong I have done, what imprecation I have uttered, and what untruth I have spoken."

Rig Veda (*c*.1700–1000 BC)

SORROW WILL PASS

"Soon the ice will melt, and the blackbirds sing along the river which he frequented, as pleasantly as ever."

Henry David Thoreau (1817–1862)

CLEANSING WATERS

WATER CLEANSES. THE PUREST WATERS ARE OFTEN THOUGHT TO BE DEW AND SPRING WATER — BUT ALSO RAIN. KEY CHARACTERISTICS ARE TRANSPARENCY (NO DECEPTION, NO CLOUDY EMOTIONS), AND ALSO THE POWER TO WASH AWAY STAINS AND EVEN OBSTRUCTIONS. THE SACRED WELLS OF THE CELTIC WORLD INTENSIFY THE MYSTIC POWER OF WATER AND HAVE THE ADVANTAGE, FOR THE MANDALA MEDITATOR, OF BEING CIRCULAR, AND THEREFORE SUGGESTIVE OF ETERNITY: YOU MIGHT VISUALIZE THE MANDALA ON PAGE 253 AS A WELL IF YOU CHOOSE TO. OTHER ASSOCIATIONS OF WATER INCLUDE FERTILITY AND FLUIDITY. IN TROUBLED TIMES, ASK YOURSELF WHICH OF WATER'S QUALITIES YOU NEED IN ORDER TO GET TO THE OTHER SIDE OF THE STORMY SEA UNSCATHED.

REGENERATING SUN

WHEN WE FEEL DEPLETED OF STRENGTH, WE CAN DRAW ON THE NATURAL
FORCES WITHIN, AROUND AND ABOVE US. IN THIS MANDALA, THE FIRE OF
THE SUN, THE LIGHT OF THE MOON AND THE STARS, AND THE RHYTHM OF
THE COSMOS ALL PROVIDE US WITH ALTERNATIVE SOURCES OF ENERGY.

1 Focus on the sunflower surrounded
by a glowing sun, both symbols of
vibrant life, inspiration and enthusiasm.
Feel the fiery colours raise your spirits
and your energy.

2 Take your attention to the four
phases of the moon circling the sun,
a reminder that all things have their
phases and seasons. Be reassured that
darkness makes way for light, and stale
energy for fresh inspiration.

3 Shift your focus out to encompass
the yin-yang symbol, which contains
night and day. See the value in both
aspects; observe how each rests within
the other. Let the stars illuminate your
darkness to show the path ahead. Let
worries drift by like clouds.

4 Finally, view the whole mandala.
Let the energy of the solar centre,
and its surrounds, lift your spirits and
feed your energy.

*"The art of healing comes from nature, not from the physician;
because the physician must start from nature, with an open mind."*

Paracelsus (1493–1541)

THE ALL-SEEING EYE

MANY CHALLENGES WE FACE REQUIRE US TO TAP INTO OUR DEEP
INNER WELL OF WISDOM — NOT LEAST FOR AN UNDERSTANDING
OF HOW SERIOUS THE CHALLENGE TRULY IS. TAP INTO YOUR WISE SELF
AT THE CENTRE OF THIS MANDALA TO DEAL WITH DIFFICULT SITUATIONS.

1 Focus on the pupil at the centre of the mandala. Enter its darkness and move into the quiet space where your true wisdom lies.

2 Widen your gaze to take in the whole eye: your wise self looking back at you with confidence and calm.

3 Shift your attention out to the stylized eyes, taken from ancient Egyptian art. See these as keys to your deepest knowledge and skills, which you can call on at times of need. Visualize them opening doors of perception inside yourself.

4 Finally, bring the wise animals into focus. Let your innate wisdom tell you how to use the owl's ability to see from all angles and guide you in how to be strong and dignified, like the elephant.

*"We do not receive wisdom, we must discover it for ourselves, after
a journey through the wilderness that no one else can make ..."*

Marcel Proust (1871–1922)

SIGHT AND INSIGHT

THE EYE IS A PORTAL THROUGH WHICH WISDOM ENTERS, WHETHER FROM OBSERVATION OR FROM READING. ITS PUPIL IS A WELL, A MANDALA, AN UNFATHOMABLE DEPTH. TRADITIONALLY, SYMBOLS OF SIGHT RANGE FROM THE EYE OF HORUS (DENOTING THE WISDOM OF THE FALCON SKY GOD IN ANCIENT EGYPT) TO THE EYE OF VISHNU IN INDIA, WHOSE EVERY BLINK IS THOUGHT TO MARK THE PASSING OF AN EPOCH. EYES, THE WINDOWS OF THE SOUL, MAY BE ACCOMPANIED BY A PSYCHIC "THIRD EYE" AT THE FOREHEAD, ASSOCIATED WITH INTUITION AND WISE PERCEPTION. THE EYE IS LINKED WITH THE "I" THAT OBSERVES THE WORLD. IN MEDITATION, YOU ENCOURAGE THIS "I" TO LOOK INSIDE, TRAWLING YOUR DEEPEST INNER REALMS FOR THE KEYS TO SELF-KNOWLEDGE.

WAYS OF SEEING

"How can the divine Oneness be seen?
... If you are willing to be lived by it, you will
see it everywhere, even in the most ordinary things."

Tao Te Ching (6th century BC)

A FLASH OF LIGHT

"Intuition is the clear conception
of the whole at once."

Johann Kaspar Lavater (1741–1801)

PHOENIX RISING

THE HUMAN BODY HAS AMAZING POWERS OF SELF-HEALING
(JUST THINK OF A CUT IN THE SKIN) AND REGENERATION. FINDING
CALM IN MEDITATION CAN HELP US TO DEAL EVEN WITH SERIOUS
ILLNESSES AND CERTAINLY WITH STRESS, LISTLESSNESS AND DEPRESSION.
PHOENIX-LIKE WE CAN RISE ANEW FROM DAMAGE.

1 Contemplate the rising phoenix, symbol of your invincible spirit. Imagine it giving you its blessing, the feathery tips of its wings stroking your body with slow, healing magic.

2 Focus on the apple, an emblem of your trust in nature, and the clusters of fruit that represent your practical plan for well-being (make one in advance, perhaps including good diet and exercise).

3 Now find the white dove that represents all that inspires you – faith in nature, hope for the future, belief in the spirit.

4 Finally, meditate on the triangle with a spot at its centre – the emblem of elemental fire. This is where your fears and your sickness burn away, and you can find liberation. Shed your anxieties as you meditate on the core of your invulnerable true self.

"He who sings frightens away his ills."

Miguel de Cervantes (1547–1616)

THE FIREBIRD

THE PHOENIX SYMBOLIZES REGENERATION. ACCORDING TO A LEGEND THAT AROSE IN HELIOPOLIS, ANCIENT CENTRE OF EGYPTIAN SUN WORSHIP, THE PHOENIX WAS A MALE BIRD OF GREAT LONGEVITY — 500 YEARS OR MORE. ONLY ONE OF THESE BEAUTIFUL CREATURES COULD LIVE AT ANY ONE TIME. WHEN ITS END DREW NEAR, THE PHOENIX FACED THE RISING SUN IN THE EAST, BUILT ITSELF A NEST OF AROMATIC TWIGS AND SANG SO ENCHANTINGLY THAT EVEN THE SUN GOD PAUSED ON HIS JOURNEY. AS A SPARK FROM THE SUN IGNITED ITS NEST, THE PHOENIX, ENGULFED IN FLAMES, DIED AND WAS BORN ANEW. IT THEN FLEW OFF CARRYING ITS ASHES AS AN OFFERING TO THE SUN GOD. THE SYMBOL HAS BEEN ASSOCIATED WITH CHRIST'S RESURRECTION AND WITH THE AWAKENING FAITH OF SPIRITUAL INITIATES.

THE PROMISE OF RENEWAL

"As the same person inhabits the body through childhood, youth and old age, so too at the time of death he attains another body."

The Bhagavad Gita (*c.*5th century BC)

PRECIOUS FUEL

"The fire that burns is the fire that gives life, and sometimes the best fuel is something precious to us."

Giuseppe Maraspini (1845–1910)

DRAGON POWER

A DRAGON REPRESENTS THE PASSIONATE ENERGY WITHIN YOU, OFFERING PROTECTION FROM DANGER AND STANDING GUARD OVER YOUR INNER NATURE. WHEN YOU FEEL THREATENED, USE THIS MANDALA TO CALL UPON YOUR INNER GUARDIAN TO GIVE YOU COURAGE AND KEEP YOU SAFE.

1 Meditate on the spiral at the centre of the mandala, symbolizing your life energy. Notice that it lies within the protective shell of an egg. Feel this shell nurturing and cradling your bottomless reserves of energy.

2 Now tap into the power of the dragon, which makes you strong and protects you. This is the strength that you summon from your energy reserves when you are under pressure.

3 The dragon is in a ring, with its tail to its mouth — emblem of the indivisible spirit. This provides all the energy you need to be yourself and protect yourself — if you have enough energy, these are the same thing.

4 Beyond the diamond of protective flames, gaze at the open clam shells with pearls on them — dragon power makes you feel safe enough to open up to others.

"For an impenetrable shield, stand inside yourself."

Henry David Thoreau (1817–1862)

THE CIRCLE OF RENEWAL

THE OURUBOROS IS A SNAKE OR DRAGON THAT SWALLOWS ITS TAIL TO FORM THE SHAPE OF A CIRCLE. THE CREATURE IS INTEGRAL TO MANY CREATION MYTHS, WHERE IT IS DESCRIBED AS ENCIRCLING THE WORLD, HOLDING OUR GLOBE IN A PROTECTIVE EMBRACE. IT SYMBOLIZES PRIMORDIAL UNITY, SELF-SUFFICIENCY AND THE CYCLES OF NATURE — MOST OBVIOUSLY THE REGENERATING FORCE OF CREATION THAT EMERGES OUT OF DESTRUCTION. THE OURUBOROS REPRESENTS AN UNFOLDING PROCESS OF RENEWAL: THE ALPHA AND OMEGA, THE BEGINNING AND THE END. ALL THAT IS KNOWN AND UNKNOWN IS CONTAINED WITHIN ITS AMBIT, AND IN SOME IMAGES THE EGG THAT IT HOLDS BETWEEN ITS CLAWS SYMBOLIZES THE PHILOSOPHER'S STONE, THE FOUNT OF ALL KNOWLEDGE.

WORLD WITHOUT END

*"I am Alpha and Omega, the beginning and
the ending ... which is, and which was,
and which is to come ..."*

Revelation (1:8)

ENDLESS RENEWAL

"Still ending, and beginning still."

William Cowper (1731–1800)

GOLDEN CROSS

IT IS SAID THAT FEW OF US KNOW OUR OWN STRENGTH. WE MOST OFTEN FIND IT WHEN WE LEAST EXPECT IT, IN TESTING TIMES. IN THIS MANDALA WE DRAW POWER FROM THE UNIVERSAL SYMBOL OF THE CROSS, OVERLAID WITH THE ROSE, IN A COMPOSITE EMBLEM OF POTENT HEALING.

1 Focus on the rose in the centre of the mandala. Recognize its beauty. This is your inner strength – delicate yet powerful. Let the potency of your inner rose unfold.

2 Now gaze at the cross, where matter and spirit meet. Your greatest strength comes as you access the point of connection. Visualize yourself centred and solid, strengthened by indestructible spirit.

3 Shift your attention to the rays that burst out from the cross. They represent your inner starlight, a unique destiny that illuminates your life – a refulgence that gives your time on Earth glorious meaning.

4 Finally, look at the small roses on the circular perimeter. Strength needs only to be felt, not displayed: you can show the gentler side of yourself instead, even in hard times.

"A man's true state of power and riches is to be in himself."

Henry Ward Beecher (1813–1887)

A UNIVERSAL SYMBOL

ONE OF OUR MOST ANCIENT AND UNIVERSAL SYMBOLS, THE CROSS
RESONATES WITH PROFOUD MEANINGS, MAKING IT RICH AS AN OBJECT
OF MEDITATION. PRINCIPALLY, IT DENOTES THE INTERSECTION OF
EARTHLY LIFE AND SPIRIT — AND IN THIS RESPECT MAY BE SEEN
AS A SIMPLIFICATION OF THE TREE OF LIFE. A CROSS CAN ALSO
REPRESENT THE FOUR DIRECTIONS AND THE FOUR SEASONS — THE
ENERGY OF NATURE'S LIFE-FORCE. THE ANCIENT EGYPTIAN *ANKH*
(A CROSS WITH A LOOP AT THE TOP INSTEAD OF THE UPPER ARM)
AND THE CELTIC CROSS ENCOMPASSED BY A CIRCLE BOTH HAVE
ASSOCIATIONS WITH ETERNAL LIFE — CELEBRATING (IN AN OBVIOUS
LINK WITH THE CHRISTIAN CROSS) THE TRIUMPH OVER DEATH
AND SUFFERING, AND THE ENDURING NATURE OF THE SPIRIT.

SPIRITUAL ORIENTATION

"As a needle turns to the north, so I turn to the spirit and all my fleshly being knows where truth lies."

Juliana Pereira (1895–1976)

THE CRUX OF NOW

"Embrace the cross of the present, the eternal now where illusions perish in a bountiful fire."

Kostas Laskari (1910–2001)

THE JAWS OF THE LION

IN THE ROYAL LION HUNT OF ANTIQUITY, COMMON IN WESTERN ASIA, THE
KILLING OF THE GOD-LIKE SOLAR LION GUARANTEED THE CONTINUATION
OF LIFE. WE SOMETIMES NEED TO SUPPRESS WHAT IS MOST OBVIOUSLY
POWERFUL IN OURSELVES TO REACH A DEEPER SOURCE OF STRENGTH.

1 Be brave and look into the mouth
of the lion. This is the Other, yet also
something found in ourselves – our
animal nature, from which our instincts
stem (as distinct from our intuitions,
which are more refined).

2 Now let your gaze rest on the lion's
teeth. You have your weapons if you
choose to use them. Yet you also have
love, wisdom and faith, which are likely
to be more effective.

3 Look at the lion's head. A lion can
roar loudly, but the wisdom of our inner
silence is likely to serve us better than
a show of aggression or an attention-
seeking cry.

4 Finally, take your attention to the
battlements around the lion's head: they
will keep the fortress of your soul safe
from harm. You have as much presence
in the world as the mighty lion, and a
nobler destiny.

"Bravery is stability, not of legs and arms, but of courage and the soul."

Michel de Montaigne (1533–1592)

LOTUS HARVEST

THE LOTUS STANDS FOR PURITY AND ENLIGHTENMENT, THE ABILITY OF
THE SELF TO GROW OUT OF FLESHLY ORIGINS AND BLOOM WITH SPIRITUAL
BEAUTY. THE MUD MAY EVOKE TRANSIENCE, THE INEVITABILITY THAT
YOUTH WILL FADE; BUT WISDOM COUNSELS US TO ACCEPT AND REJOICE.

1 Focus on the lotus at the centre of the mandala. It has opened to beauty, despite its humble origins in mud; and this beauty comes from the very core of the self.

2 Shift your focus to the blue of the lake water shimmering with reflections. This is a place to bathe and find calm, confident in the knowledge of your spiritual maturity. Feel the cool waters refreshing you.

3 Gaze at the six lotus blossoms around the central flower. Let the seven blooms drift in your consciousness as you relax in pleasant thoughts. Time passes but the moment gives ample space for contentment.

4 Finally, look at the corn stalks in the corners of the square, symbolizing the growing self. Sink into the peace that comes with this knowledge of your spiritual harvest.

"The harvest treasures all now gathered in, beyond the range of storms."

James Thomson (1700–1748)

PURE DEPTHS

"Simply always let go and make your heart empty and open. Be like the stillness of water, like the clarity of a mirror."

Ta Hui (1088–1163)

ROOT AND BLOOM

"My mind is a flower, meditation my roots."

Ahmet Nedim (1681–1730)

NATURE AND SPIRIT

WHEN APPLIED TO THE MIND AND THE SPIRIT, AS DISTINCT FROM THE BODY, HEALING IS MORE THAN A METAPHOR, BECAUSE OUR BODIES ARE NOT THE ONLY PART OF US THAT CAN SUFFER ILL HEALTH — OUR INNER SELF CAN TOO, AND SO CAN OUR RELATIONSHIPS WITH OTHERS, WITH THE COSMOS AND WITH THE ONE. NATURE PROVIDES AN ORGANIC PHARMACY THAT EQUIPS US TO HEAL THESE INTANGIBLE RIFTS AND IMBALANCES. JUST AS HERBS CAN FIX OUR BODILY ILLS, THE IMAGERY OF NATURE, TAKEN INTERNALLY, CAN WORK ON OUR MENTAL AND SPIRITUAL ISSUES AND PROMOTE GENTLE REPAIR. THIS IS AS UNOBTRUSIVE AS HEALING GETS: WE JUST TAKE INTO CONCIOUSNESS A FLORAL MANDALA, OR A REAL FLOWER, AND ALLOW OURSELVES TO BE WORKED ON BY THE BEST MEDICINE IN THE COSMOS.

Natural Mandalas

The mandala is a representation of a truth that lies all around us and deep inside ourselves. Thus, nature, the creative life-force, is the ultimate mandala, one that reveals itself moment by moment if we pause and allow ourselves to appreciate what we see. Nature is full of patterns and harmony: the light and shade cast by sunlight, the trees against the skyline, the dome of the heavens, the stones under our feet, the rain on the windowpane, the wind in the hills, the line of the seashore, the rhythm of the seasons, the ease of animals in movement or repose — everything speaks to us of the mandalas of creation. And there is ample beauty here to soothe the spirit.

*"Nature is full of genius, full of the divinity; so that not a
snowflake escapes its fashioning hand."*
Henry David Thoreau (1817–1862)

*"On a cosmic scale, our life is insignificant, yet this brief period
when we appear in the world is the time in which all
meaningful questions arise."*
Paul Ricœur (1913–2005)

PATTERNS IN NATURE

A mandala is a pattern or device on which to meditate. The term is especially associated with the elaborate designs used for meditation in the Tantric Buddhist tradition of Tibet – complex hierarchies of imagery within a circular frame, charged with a symbolism that invariably strikes modern-day Westerners as profoundly esoteric. Essentially these devices represent the palace of the gods, in countless variations. By absorbing the palace of the mandala into his or her own consciousness, the meditator re-orientates their worldview, as their inner focus shifts from the distractions of the outer world to the virtues of self-awareness, wisdom and compassion.

Modern mandalas are often designed to be more accessible to today's seekers, thanks to a broader repertoire of symbolism – for example, such motifs as the Celtic endless knot, which represents the perpetual flow of time and the journey of the pilgrim; and the mud-transcending lotus, suggestive of pure, undefiled spirit.

Nature, the creative life-force, is in many ways the ultimate mandala. The Tantric mandalas of Buddhism depict the elements and the cycle of birth, life and death – both primal forces of nature – together with various deities and demons. Such devices were carefully designed by sages to open up the seeker's perceptions. However, it is possible to achieve a similar effect using nature's actual phenomena as an object of meditation. Nature's symbolism is apparently simple yet in many ways profoundly intricate. By dwelling on the vast interconnectedness of all living things we can access important insights.

In nature, mandalas can be seen wherever we choose to look. The whorl of a shell, the tightly furled petals of a rose, the age-rings within the trunk of a tree, the patterns made by leaves against the sky – all of these, and more, are portals to a realm that transcends the mundane. Each object of focus becomes a symbol, opening up the mind to a greater understanding of life. We attain a deep knowledge of our place in the grand scheme of the cosmos – a knowledge that is intuitive rather than intellectual. We perceive ourselves as a single strand in the web of life, yet paradoxically this gives us an experience of unity. We know ourselves to be both the weaver and the web. The sense of separation that is the cause of so many of humanity's problems is dissolved by the understanding that we are a single cell in the body of life itself, nurtured and supported in our growth, and capable of fully realizing our potential.

NATURAL MANDALAS AND MEDITATION

As we previously explained, the shape considered to be most potent in a mandala is the circle. This is used in all mandalas, and other shapes such as the square and triangle are secondary to it. The circle represents the endless cycle of life, with no beginning and no end. The space within the circle symbolizes the inner realm, a magical space enclosed and protected by the periphery. The still, central point from which the circumference is measured represents the self, the spiritual hub that drives the wheel of life in perpetual motion.

In nature the circle can be found in the sun, the moon and the planets. It is the defining shape of fruits such as oranges and cherries. It gazes back at us through the iris and pupil of the eye. It can also be seen in the centre of a flower and the head of a mushroom. Meditating on the circle in nature's mandalas can bring us to a realization of wholeness, harmony and inner peace. A variation on the circle is the spiral, in which the circular motion uncoils like a spring. Instead of converging on a closed meeting point, each section moves on to a new phase, reminding us of the progression of understanding that ultimately leads to true knowledge – the deep spiritual self. Then there is the oval, which like the circle is enclosed, and is a symbol of birth and renewal. These are all important shapes in nature. The square, by contrast, symbolizes containment: it creates a sense of solidity and security which "holds" the energy of the symbols placed within it. All the shapes within a mandala help to enhance the power of its individual symbols, and bring about an expansion of consciousness when we meditate on them.

The aim of meditation is to still the mind, and mandalas are such a powerful tool for meditation because the mind creates its strongest associations through visual imagery. If you think of a favourite flower, or a constellation, or a pagoda beside a lake, an image will immediately arise in your mind. Being intensely visual, and framed within a dynamic design, a mandala, once absorbed into your mind, works subtle changes on your mental state, which then filter through to influence your feelings and emotions. This can generate a heightened state of awareness in which insights come to the surface and your perceptions are enhanced.

NATURE AS SPIRITUAL REFRESHMENT

For centuries we have felt a sense of spiritual sustenance when observing a glorious sunset, or a distant lake shore, or the gentle undulation of grasses in the wind. Our primitive ancestors no doubt had more basic feelings that we will never be able to recapture. But certainly today, contemplating nature has a healing and calming effect on the senses and on the soul.

Nature as spiritual refreshment is a topic in the literature of many different cultures. In ancient Greece the philosopher Aristotle stated that "In all things of nature there is something of the marvellous." The Bible tells how Jesus spent forty days and nights in the desert, wrestling with his inner demons, which culminated in his emergence as a great teacher. The German poet, scientist and thinker Johann Wolfgang von Goethe (1749–1832) considered that whenever the best was attained in human nature, this was a reflection of the beauty and wholeness of the universe. In his scientific writings he insists that it is not always necessary to look for reasons behind the phenomena of the natural world, that sometimes it is more appropriate simply to appreciate them for what they are. Jacob Boehme (1575–1624), a Teutonic philosopher and mystic, spoke of recognizing God in every blade of grass. The poetry of the thirteenth-century Sufi master Rumi describes the life of the spirit as being contained and expressed within all aspects of the natural realm. World literature is rich in references to nature as nurturer of the soul.

Nature is refreshingly uncomplicated. Like the spirit, it transcends boundaries, and is not subject to divisions of culture or creed. A flower never wishes to be a tree: it accepts the bending wind, the nourishing sun and rain, and willingly offers its nectar to passing bees and butterflies. The rhythms of life are accepted without question by plants and animals, and so we can learn from nature a great deal about how to flow with the tides in our own lives by refusing to participate in a futile struggle against the inevitable. Anyone who tunes in to nature understands that all things are part of the flow of the universe, and have their own unique place within an overall interdependence. And because everything that exists naturally is an expression of the sacred, in nature we recognize an infinite power.

Of course, the other key factor that links nature with inner refreshment lies in the contrast between nature and society: nature can be a way of seclusion, a place to be alone. In the East, especially in China and Tibet, monasteries are frequently sited in remote areas, high in the mountains. This allows the seeker of spiritual truths to be set apart from the everyday dramas of non-secular life. Living quietly and peacefully, with respect for the environment and its gifts and challenges, we can purify our minds, allowing the spiritual self to shine through. Many small, self-sustaining communities, based on values of harmony with nature, downsizing and charitable involvement with local people, attest to the appeal of this idea.

Yet, of course, the experience of tranquil seclusion in nature can often be obtained without distancing oneself too much from normal, social routines. You can sit in the countryside and watch nature astir around you – worms making their air-tunnels, insects helping plants to pollinate, birds prospecting twigs for their nests, depending on the time of year. Or you can sit by a river, a lake or the sea, and watch the flow of water, the stuff of life. For a more awe-inspiring view you can lie on the ground on a clear night and observe the overhead procession of the stars. Refreshment for the spirit is all around us, and even city-dwellers may find it readily in a park or garden, if only they are willing to look.

NATURE AS PURE BEING

Nature expresses the pure and harmonious state of being that is sought through meditation. In the process of accepting ourselves as we are in nature, we become aware of the simple progression of birth, death and regeneration that is present in all forms of life on our planet. This awareness brings with it a profound sense of spiritual connection. The dualities of good and bad, appetite and reason, that the eighteenth-century French philosopher Jean-Jacques Rousseau considered to be the result of humanity's development from the "noble savage" to the "civilized" human being, are dissolved in the perception of all living things as an expression of spirit.

Looking at nature in the broadest perspective, we see a vast interactive system that enables the survival of life in all its forms – a great drama featuring rain and sun providing energy for growth, wind dispersing seeds, and predators ensuring a natural balance between animal species. The Gaia theory formed in the 1960s by James Lovelock views the Earth as an "intelligent", self-regulating, self-sustaining organism, constantly acting to maintain the balance necessary for survival. Just as the cells in your body each have their purpose in sustaining health, working together to create an intricate, coherent whole, so each component within nature contributes to the good of the entire organism within the complex web of life. We ourselves belong to this web, and to see this is to relish and enjoy, rather than fear, our overlapping cycles of living and dying.

Nature is not only pure being, it also presents to us in infinitely various forms the *beauty* of pure being. From natural beauty we derive inspiration and inner nourishment. At its most extreme this

STONE CIRCLES

One of the deepest connections humankind can make with nature is to tune in to the dynamic energies or force-fields that lie within the Earth. In various cultures, from Native North American to Celtic European, certain areas of landscape have been seen as reservoirs of power – places where the forces of nature are especially concentrated and potent.

Understanding this, our distant ancestors erected standing stones, dolmens and stone circles to harness this natural energy, which they then used in spiritual ceremonies aimed at strengthening and unifying the tribe.

It would not stretch credulity too far to suggest that prehistoric stone circles are three-dimensional mandalas placed within a landscape. When you walk among such structures, or contemplate an aerial view of their mysterious patterns, it is impossible not to be impressed by their silent power.

shades into awe, convincing us
of life's richness, its spiritual value.
A feeling of rightness and perfection
elevates us to a sense of communion
with the creative force that gives rise
to and lies within all these manifold
forms. By attuning ourselves to this
feeling, we step out of our everyday
selves, becoming not merely a witness
or participant, but something far
more significant – a kind of natural
stakeholder in beauty, in meaning, in joy.

The sense of joy, although requiring
deep meditation to be fully accessed,
can be felt in a more diluted way by
appreciating nature outwardly in various
activities. Walking or hiking, swimming,
climbing, or just experiencing the
breath of a breeze on naked skin,
all bring about a heightening of the
senses. This helps to remove the mind
from the problems and distractions of

everyday life, and its uncomfortable
subscription to role play, power struggles,
the assertion and competition of egos.
Sitting in silent contemplation of a
natural scene or feature enables you to
pierce the wildness, to move beyond the
outward forms to unity and universality,
to knowledge of the simplicity of the
pure intelligence that lies behind
the forms, and to an understanding
of infinity.

NATURE AND RELAXATION

Deep contemplation, and even more so
meditation, requires conscious mental
engagement. However, nature can also
work more subtle effects on our state of
mind, relaxing us to an experience of
peace without our having to make any
conscious mental effort at all. Simply
gazing at a green or rocky landscape,

or looking out to an azure sea, or being aware of clouds drifting endlessly overhead while we are involved in some physical activity (anything from playing with our children to mending a fence or setting up an easel for painting), can give us a sense of natural belonging.

The typical shapes found in nature, which complement each other so well, have a restful effect. Green, of course, is a famously restful colour, valued by actors for their pre- or post-performance unwinding in the "green room", and the greeny blues or greys of the ocean, or the view of a forest, can put us at ease in a similar way. However, the reds, browns and ochres of a desert can be no less soothing in the right light. Horizontals in the landscape tend to soothe – think of a tranquil pool or the ocean's horizon. On the other hand, verticals, such as tall trees or mountains, inspire.

NATURE AND INSPIRATION

Many people have chosen to surround themselves with nature to nourish their thoughts. Carl Gustav Jung (1875–1961), the Swiss-German psychiatrist whose ideas opened up the landscape of the mind and illuminated knowledge of the inner life, was a champion of nature's healing power. Jung insisted on living near water, which he considered to be a symbol of the collective unconscious and of intuitive wisdom. He was deeply influenced by the Romantic poetry of Blake, Wordsworth, Coleridge and Goethe, all of whom wrote of the soul's need for the beauty of the natural world. Typically, according to the Romantic worldview, there is no separation between nature and spirit.

However, this deep affinity was appreciated long before the nineteenth century. The sixth-century BC Chinese philosopher Lao Tzu, whose *Tao Te Ching* has inspired so many people, linked the natural world to human attributes, and wrote his stanzas as instructions for right living. He wrote about the Tao, the mysterious, all-pervasive life-force. By attuning to nature, it is possible to perceive this life-force flowing through nature's many forms. "The highest good is like water," he wrote. "Water gives life to the ten thousand things and does not strive. It flows in places men reject, and so is like the Tao."

CALMING WATER

In psychology, water symbolizes the unconscious mind – the thoughts, feelings, urges and memories that are buried deep within the psyche. This includes the collective unconscious, the imprinted inherited memories and archetypal patterns of generations, which form a blueprint for the "group mind" of humanity. Water has always been associated with the primordial fluid from which all living things are born. The magical elixir, which in countless myths has the power to bestow immortality, bring the dead back to life and cure all diseases, has its natural analogy in water. In Greek myth the souls of the dead drank the waters of Lethe, a river in Hades (the underworld), to bring about forgetfulness of all that had gone before, so that they would not mourn the loved ones they had left behind. Water is also the basis of the Fountain of Youth, sought by heroes in many myths. In magic, still water in a puddle, a lake or a bowl is used for scrying (a form of divination), as it allows the mind to settle and see images from deep within the unconscious.

But quite apart from these symbolic associations, water has purely physical properties that make it psychologically important to us. If you sit by a lake on a still day, the perfect flatness of the surface of the water has a soothing effect, helping to slow the mind into a state of meditative calmness. Watch a fish come to the surface, or cast a stone into the water. Ripples will radiate in an outward flow, creating circles within circles — a natural mandala revealing how stillness can accommodate motion and change. At the same time, the reflections of clouds or the surrounding landscape on the water's surface create dreamlike images that can draw the mind inward.

A river embodies the flow of the life-force, swirling around obstacles, creating a complex pattern of eddies and currents. It moves inexorably from its source to the sea. The mind shares this compulsion to integrate, being drawn toward unifying the diverse parts of ourselves with the greater whole. The sounds of moving water are relaxing and hypnotic, so it is not surprising that meditation music often includes the murmur of a stream or river.

THE LIVING FOREST

We have explored the universal and cultural associations of water, which come into play in some of the natural mandalas in this book. In contrast to water's essential simplicity, the forest is a complex network of interdependent life forms — but still rich in meaning for the meditator. The quality of light in a forest is soft and diffused, often with dappled shade where the sun's rays play through foliage. This greenish light coupled with a hushed stillness can almost make you feel you are underwater. Yet, if you listen, the forest is not silent. Sounds of rustling foliage, snuffles and squeaks of small creatures, and high-pitched bird calls all form part of the sensory experience. The rich scent of leaves and bark, earth and loam, awakens the olfactory sense, releasing memories and recalling associated emotions. All these factors combine to create an ever-changing three-dimensional mandala that takes the mind away from its routine chatter. The forest embodies shelter or refuge, yet it also holds an atmosphere of mystery that enables you to attune yourself more clearly to the infinite mystery of the spiritual self.

Hermits and sages in many spiritual stories have retreated to the forest to experience the simplicity of living in the wild. Within the forest can be found all that is needed to sustain life: shelter, fuel, food. In the deciduous forest nature's cycles are easily seen. By meditating on, say, a forest leaf or an acorn we can open up a pathway that leads to our own still centre.

CLOUDS AND THOUGHTS

The sky is our gateway to the infinite spaces of the universe. At a human level, it can be likened to the vast, unexplored areas of the mind. By extension, the clouds are like our thoughts, which arise, drift across the field of view, join with others and then dissolve into the boundless silence of the spiritual self. If you look up at the sky, you will feel as though you are rising into it, floating beyond the confines of your bodily self. Cloud meditation enables you to drift, light-headed, toward a heightened awareness of your place in a universe that is beyond our powers of measurement or even imagination.

Cloud formations can make interesting quasi-mandalas – whether rolling cumulus, with its soft hills and valleys; the ripples of a mackerel sky, like fish-scales; wispy cirrus, like strands of silky hair in the upper stratosphere; or dark, rain-bearing nimbostratus, which wraps us in a blanket, and reminds us that water is the source of life.

When you use clouds as a basis for meditation, the secret is to "go with the flow" of the cloud formations as the wind breaks them up into an ever-changing parade of abstractions. Soften your vision, and look at one particular cloud, or section of the cloudscape, making this the centre of your awareness. Drift with it and into it, and feel yourself

becoming lighter as you liberate your mind from Earthly cares and concerns. Breathe gently and easily, and feel your body relax as your mind rises to meet the cloud. Be aware of the sky without attaching any conscious thoughts to what you see – without making any judgments or comparisons.

✤ ✤ ✤

Part of the point of meditating on nature is that we ourselves are an intrinsic part of the natural world. The only division betwen ourselves and our natural surroundings is the frontiers of self and consciousness, which meditation dissolves. By projecting ourselves into nature, via a natural mandala, we affirm the unity of existence. The mandalas in this book draw upon traditional symbolism associated in various cultures with natural features, the most important of which are profiled on pages 302-317.

THE MEDITATION GARDEN

A garden can be an expression of your connection with nature. Spiritual gardens may appear in many forms, depending on geographical factors, the purpose of the garden, and the cultural tradition it reflects. Although a garden is usually considered to be a way of taming and civilizing nature, leaving a wild area where nature is allowed to take its course can provide an appealing contrast.

You can plan a garden specifically with meditation in mind. Any individual

SAND MANDALAS

In Buddhist Tibet, impermanent mandalas, known as *kilkhors*, are created using flowers, dyed grains of rice, crushed precious stones and coloured grains of sand. In a spiritual ceremony called the *Kalachakra Initiation*, the mandala is painstakingly laid out in areas of different-coloured sands. The purpose of the ceremony is to bring about personal and world peace, and to remind each participant of the transitory nature of the material world. Afterwards, the mandala is swept away until no trace remains.

You can create your own sand mandala on a beach, close to the shore. Begin at the centre of the mandala and work outward, using your finger, a shell or a small stone to etch a symmetrical design into the sand. You can choose motifs from mandalas in this book for your sand mandala, or create your own design using geometric shapes, circles or spirals. When you have finished, sit back and meditate on your mandala. Then wait for the tide to come in and wash it away.

area can be laid out like a mandala — as a special place in which to celebrate the magnificent creations of nature and allow the mind to open itself up to beauty all around. Pattern can be provided in the planting scheme or in the hard surfaces — for example, an alternation of stone paving and herringbone brickwork or gravel. If you wish, you can treat the whole garden as a mandala, which you access either by sitting and meditating in it, or by meditatively walking around a particular route. Paths, with ornaments used as punctuation points, can be planned to guide the eye. Water features will provide sound and movement.

The Zen garden, in the Japanese Buddhist tradition, is a customized meditation space. Simple to an extreme, Zen gardens use "sand", which is actually crushed granite, in shades of white-grey to beige. In the most common, dry-style Zen gardens, sculptured rocks are used to create mountains and islands, each one usually in the approximate shape of a tortoise or a crane — creatures known for their longevity. Bridges cross the "seas" of sand from one rocky island to another, and are pleasing to the eye. Ornaments act as focal points and help to provide a sense of perspective.

A Chinese garden is composed of an area of rocks, plants and water, surrounded by buildings and walls, which provide decorative architectural structures and enhance the effect of the internal design. The organization of the Chinese garden is aimed at promoting a feeling of relaxation and well-being. It is rigorously planned to include the elements, expressed through plants, water, stones and architecture, with a

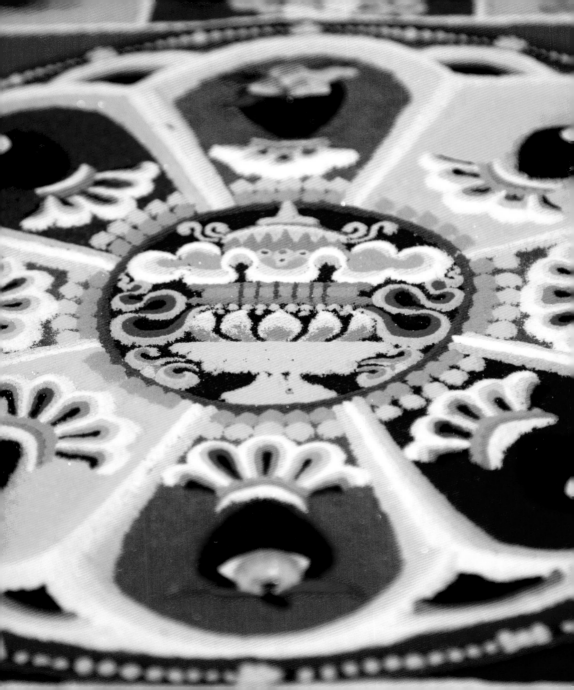

balance of yin and yang in a harmonious design that employs unusual perspective and a great deal of metaphorical meaning. Instead of imitating nature, the creator of a Chinese garden manipulates the components of nature to create contrast and arouse the emotions. Traditional Chinese plants such as peonies, chrysanthemums, flowering plum trees and bamboo bring colour and texture into the garden, as well as symbolic meaning.

MAKING A MINIATURE ZEN GARDEN

Although many people who live in cities have no garden, a number of us have a balcony or access to a roof terrace, where we can capture the essence of a Zen garden by creating our own miniature version in a container.

Choose a selection of small flowers, shrubs and dwarf trees and place them in a window box or other suitable receptacle. Select plants that will flourish in your climate. If you live in a temperate zone, you may wish to feature plants which, in Japan, are traditionally associated with the end of the old year and the beginning of the new, such as plum and pine trees (both are available in miniature). Or if you live in hot, semi-arid conditions, you can use flowering succulent plants, such as cacti, as a basis for your garden.

Even if you have no outside space, you can still make a tiny indoor Zen garden, using, for example, a large, shallow container in which you arrange some pebbles around a bonsai tree.

Left: This Tibetan kilkhor (sand mandala) is composed of intricate lines and areas of coloured sand and stone. After a short time, the patterns are swept away to represent the transient nature of life.

TRANSCENDENTAL RETREAT

There is an important tradition of retreat that lies outside the history of monastic practice – a less institutionalized approach, which was especially important in America in the nineteenth century. A life lived in harmony with nature was proposed by the Boston Transcendentalists, a movement of progressive thinkers whose ideas stemmed from the theories of Immanuel Kant (1724–1804) and the German Transcendentalists. The Boston movement extolled the gifts and beauty of the natural world, rejected new technology, and aimed to create a new form of literature based on humankind's relationship with nature. They were educated people who chose to identify themselves with the harmony and simplicity of the natural world, and to adopt a different perspective on spirituality, religion, art and politics from that provided by the general social mores of their time. The Transcendental Club was formed in Boston, Massachusetts, in 1836, and attracted a growing number of writers and intellectuals. Ralph Waldo Emerson, who hosted the meetings, gave a succinct summary of the credo: "Nature is loved by what is best in us." Henry David Thoreau, Margaret Fuller, Bronson Alcott and his daughter Louisa May Alcott, and William Ellery Channing the younger, are the best-known members, and lived near Boston, in Concord. Of these, Emerson was the most celebrated during his lifetime, although Thoreau's work is now of equal renown, and he is hailed as America's first environmentalist.

Emerson offered Thoreau a plot of land at Walden Pond, less than two miles from Concord, and there he lived on and off for two years in a cabin built with his own hands. In his book, *Walden*, Thoreau described his experiences through the changing seasons, and put forward his ideas about living close to nature, retreating from the world and rejecting the superficialities of civilization. The purpose of this experimental retreat was to live fully attuned to the natural world, and to drink deep of the bounty of nature, while also refraining from leaving an indelible impression on the landscape.

The Transcendentalists, whose values stemmed from the ideal of living in harmony with the natural world, by extension campaigned for a just balance in society, the abolition of slavery and rights for women. Combining mysticism and philosophy, they promoted the supremacy of intuition over reason, with nature as an inspiration and guide to the life of the spirit. The influence of the Transcendentalists has been pronounced: many modern-day communes, with their various degrees of eco-consciousness, owe a great deal – even indirectly – to the ideas of Emerson, Thoreau and their collaborators.

You do not have to live in a log cabin or throw away your telephone to adopt some Transcandentalist principles. Simply affirming that you will not allow yourself to be directed by the opinions of others and living by your own standards is a good start. Spending less time in front of the computer or the television and more time interacting with real people and with the natural, non-virtual world is essential. Take the time to experience the wonder of the Earth's manifold ecosystems.

TREES

Trees are powerful conduits for life-energy on our planet. They process carbon dioxide into oxygen so that we can breathe; the humus from their decaying leaves enriches the ground; and they also provide habitats for birds, animals and insects. Rainforests are essential for the planet's rainfall, which of course is the source of our drinking water. Myths involving trees are abundant, and some of us still "touch wood" for good luck.

In Druid lore, each tree has its own personality and symbol, and governs a month of the year. The Druids' alphabet, known as "Ogham", consisted of 25 characters, each encoding an aspect of tree wisdom. Groves were considered to be natural temples – places of meditation, contemplation, wisdom and healing. Entering a grove or wood, with its diversity of trees and plant life, the Druid could associate each tree and plant with many different signifiers – a number, a month, a deity, a colour, a star, an animal and a mineral. These associations could enable a kind of cross-pollination of the mind and the senses, as well as providing a workable memory system. To the Druids and nature-worshippers all trees are sacred, and each has a specific symbolism.

There is also a great deal of tree lore outside the Western tradition. To take just one notable example, pine trees in the Far East symbolize longevity, purity, health and abundance. Like the cedar, the pine was linked with incorruptibility and tended to be planted around Chinese graves. From its resin came the mushrooms upon which Taoist immortals fed. The box, opposite, gives examples of common

TREE LORE

Cultures from all ages and all parts of the world have ascribed symbolic associations to different species of tree.

Almond Divine light (Biblical lands).

Apple Marriage, fertility, good health (Europe).

Birch A benevolent, protective tree in northern Europe. Used as the central pole in a shamanic yurt (tent) in Mongolia and Siberia to symbolize our ascent to the spirit world.

Cedar Tree of life (Sumeria), representing power and immortality.

Cypress Symbolizes death and mourning in the West, but longevity and immortality in the East.

Fig The sacred tree in many regions, with associations of fertility. In Buddhism, a symbol of moral teaching and immortality (the Buddha achieved enlightenment beneath a Bodhi fig).

Hazel Wisdom, prophecy (northern Europe). Eating hazelnuts is said to open the mind, and the twigs are used for dowsing.

Oak Nobility, endurance (the West). An axial symbol of male potency and wisdom in Druid lore, though with feminine associations too.

Olive Peace, joy, victory, plenty, purity, immortality, virginity (Greece, Biblical lands).

Palm The Tree of Life in Egypt and Arabia, associated with the sun as well as fertility.

Peach Immortality, longevity, youth, marriage, protective magic (the East). The blossom represents virginity in Taoist symbolism.

Pine Immortality or longevity (the East). In a pair, marital fidelity (China and Japan). The pine cone is a symbol of masculine strength.

Willow A lunar and feminine symbol (China), and a Taoist image of strength in flexibility. The Tree of Life in Tibet.

Yew Death and rebirth (Europe). Commonly planted in churchyards, it straddles the boundary between the everyday world and the Otherworld inhabited by the spirits of the dead. Spears and shields were made from yew, for its magical properties.

A TREE MEDITATION

This meditation is one to be performed outside, in front of your chosen tree. If possible, select a tree according to the symbolism that has particular meaning for you at this time (see box, page 303). If you wish to focus on flexibility, opt for a willow tree; for kindness and protection, a birch tree. To focus on divinatory skills or altered states of awareness, a hazel; for strength and endurance, an oak.

1 Go right up close to the tree. Touch the bark: feel its texture and observe its markings. Examine the leaves, and the blossoms or fruit, if there are any, and allow the shapes, colours and patterns to become imprinted on your mind.

2 Find a comfortable place where you can sit facing the tree, with a view of the trunk and branches. Close your eyes for a moment, and visualize the tree. Imagine that it has a message for you. (Some native peoples believe that each tree is inhabited by a spirit, and you can ask for advice or guidance, which will be given if you are open and receptive). Take three deep breaths, then breathe normally.

3 Open your eyes and really look at the tree. See it as an entire organism, an eco-system for numerous life-forms. Observe how the branches spread out, the lattice they make, the way they filter the light. Draw your attention to the trunk, and focus on any prominent curves and knots. Think of the tree standing for a lifetime that is longer than your own. Look at the visible roots, and imagine them drawing nutrients and water up from the ground.

4 Absorb the image of the whole tree into your mind, and experience it there – outside you, yet inside you simultaneously. Feel the special symbolic qualities of this species absorbing themselves into your being, like water and nutrients through the tree's roots.

5 When you have finished your meditation and are ready to leave, give thanks to the tree.

trees and their symbolism in different cultures.

Trees, which embody the connection between the different layers of the cosmos, make fascinating natural mandalas. Their roots are anchored deep in the ground, and often spread to encompass the same breadth of soil that their branches take up in the sky. The roots symbolize the deep self, our constant source of nourishment, while the trunk is the conduit for the life-force, the body, which the roots sustain. The branches, with their leaves, flowers and fruit, represent the blossoming of potential into full fruition, and act as antennae for cosmic energy. By meditating on a tree (see box, opposite) you can strengthen your sense of wholeness and integrity, at the same time as drawing upon the symbolic resonance of your chosen tree.

THE ELEMENTS

In Western society we tend to consider only four elements: earth, air, fire and water. In ancient Greek culture, Aristotle (384–322 BC) attributed properties to each of these elements: earth was cold and dry; water, cold and wet; fire, hot and dry; and air, hot and wet. These four elements were encapsulated within a fifth – aether or quintessence; Buddhists also speak of this fifth element. In China, the elements are wood, fire, earth, metal and water. All the elements, of course, are vital components of life, held in a perfect balance.

You can view the elements as aspects of your internal nature, as well as external forces. Earth is the element that relates to physicality, health, material possessions and work. Psychologically the earth element keeps you grounded and brings about a sense of stability and security. Air is associated with mind, thought and intellect, as well as with communication, because air is a vehicle for sound. Water symbolizes emotion, with its propensity to flow, and to change the terrain that it encounters, while taking the shape of the container that holds it. Fire symbolizes passion and inspiration, and in its ability to transmute one substance into another it can be damaging, purifying or alchemically transformative.

The symbolism of the elements is used in Eastern healing traditions, as well as in divinatory systems such as the Tarot, the Kabbalah, the I Ching and astrology. By meditating on the elements, you can attune to their symbolic meaning

MEDITATING ON THE ELEMENTS

The ancient Greeks believed that all matter was composed of various blends of earth, air, fire and water. Thus, all substances could be transmuted into each other by creating a mixture, and varying the proportions of the elements accordingly. From $c.300$ BC to $c.$AD 1500 this theory provided the basis for alchemical study – including the quest for the mysterious "philosopher's stone", which was believed to convert base metals into gold.

All meditation is a form of alchemy – a purging away of the base components of thought and desire that distract you from your true purpose. The process distils the "gold" of wisdom and insight and brings you into contact with your essential self.

You can meditate on the elements either through visualization or with an actual example in front of you – for example, a candle or a bowl of water.

within your psyche, and use this to effect inner transformation, or bring a sense of ease and calm, or even improve health. You can choose to focus on aspects of yourself or situations in your life that need a boost. If you feel lacking in inspiration, you might decide to meditate on fire in the form of blazing logs or a candle. Meditation on a stream, a river or the sea can help you to attune to your emotions, and can enhance your intuitive faculties. If you wish to feel more grounded and practical, you can reconnect with the earth element by meditating outside in your garden, or out in the countryside. Watching the sky can put you in touch with the air element within yourself, and help you to open yourself to new horizons in your life. Even staying indoors, you can still meditate on the elements using a bowl of earth or a crystal, a glass of water, a candle and, to represent air, some incense. Smoke represents a point of transformation and can be used to symbolize the power of the elements when they work together, since it arises from a combination of earth (in the form of wood), fire and air.

The "elements" is also a term commonly used for the weather, which can be an inspiring natural mandala. Watch a storm move across the sky, and be awed by its power and intensity. Allow all your senses to become involved in this dramatic expression of natural power. Less stirring, but no less beautiful, is the whispering or roaring of the wind in the trees or blowing across water, the light rain that taps rhythms on a window, or the play of sunlight across a landscape. All these can also provide rewarding subjects for a mandala meditation.

THE NIGHT SKY

The sky has long been a focal point for myths and legends, and the setting for stories of deities and heroes of all cultures. Probably since our earliest ancestors gazed aloft, the sun, moon and stars have been objects of worship. In ancient Egypt the Milky Way was considered to be the cosmic milk that flowed from the breasts of Isis, the Great Mother. The Greeks thought of the sun as Apollo, the sun god, who rode his fiery chariot across the sky each day and retreated to the magical land of Hyperborea ("beyond the north wind") each year for the three months of winter.

Our solar system is situated on an arm of the spiralling Milky Way galaxy, which can be seen as a hazy band of white light across the celestial sphere, appearing brightest near the constellation Sagittarius, which points the way to the galactic centre. The galaxy is vast – if you could travel at the speed of light, it would take around 250,000 years to circumnavigate the Milky Way.

Symbolically the sun represents the spirit, the all-seeing eye of the self. Psychologically, it signifies growth and creativity, and is associated with the conscious mind and its capacity for discernment and evaluation. The moon symbolizes intuition, dreams, and the feeling or feminine self. Traditionally, farmers considered the new moon to be an auspicious time to sow seeds.

The night sky is patterned with dozens of constellations and thousands of individual stars. Many of the constellations, like Orion, Taurus and Ursa Major, are easy to recognize, and even the more prominent planets, such as Venus and Jupiter, should not present any difficulties. At sunrise and sunset you can see the planet Venus, which looks like a lone bright star, low above the horizon near the point where the sun rises or sets. Jupiter, when visible, is simply the largest, brightest object in the night sky apart from the moon. The Plough or Big Dipper, which is part of Ursa Major (the Great Bear), is the most easily recognizable of the constellations. In Greek myth, the great god Zeus fell in love with Callisto, a huntress, whereupon his jealous wife, the goddess Hera, turned her into a bear. Callisto's son, Arcturus, was about to kill the

HALF-MOON MEDITATION

This is an ideal meditation for city dwellers who, because of light pollution, cannot see the night sky clearly. When the moon is in its middle phase, the surface features are more clearly visible than they are on the full moon.

1 Use the moon-phase data in your diary to work out roughly the best day for a half-moon meditation. Obviously, a certain amount of luck will be needed, as cloud cover would spoil the effect – though just a few clouds passing over the moon can be incorporated into your meditation.

2 Find as peaceful a place as you can, and look up at the half-moon. Try to make out as many details as possible – ridges, craters and clouds.

3 Imagine that there is someone on the moon, gazing at the Earth. Sense your connection with all living beings throughout the universe.

4 Say goodbye to your distant friend and return your attention to the Earth.

bear, unaware that this was his mother, but Zeus quickly intervened, changed Arcturus into a smaller bear, and threw mother and son into the sky, where they remain to this day as Ursa Major and Minor. As these two constellations rotate (every 24 hours) around Polaris, the pole star, which approximates to true north, sailors could use astronomical observation to ascertain time, as well as north's direction. All these associations can be used as material for an absorbing open-air meditation for those living in the northern hemisphere when the night sky is clear.

Meditating on the constellations can help you to stretch your imagination by attuning to the relevant myths, at the same time as strengthening your awareness of the unimaginably vast spaces contained within just a tiny portion of the universe. Remember that, in the midst of all this vastness, there is a place for you, and that your life interconnects with the whole. Everything that exists is composed of the stuff of stars. We are, in truth, formed from the same elements as the sun, moon and stars – elements that came into being just moments after the birth of the universe.

LEARNING FROM WATER

Water is a gentle guide to what Taoists and Buddhists term "right living". In the story of Siddhartha, the Indian prince who became the Buddha when he meditated beneath a Bodhi tree, an old boatman named Vasudeva offered inspiration and deep understanding. He had spent all his life ferrying travellers across a river, and was attuned to its many moods and voices. Vasudeva gently suggested that Siddhartha pay attention to the water, and Siddhartha became aware of the faces and voices of all the people he loved, as they merged with the greater whole. He realized that the river was the river of life, travelled by all beings, who sang out their yearnings, sufferings and joys as the river held them within its embrace. The water raced toward its goal, the sea, joined by other rivers from all sides; and the water rose as steam and fell from the clouds as rain. This deeply felt perception enabled Siddhartha to experience unity, or nirvana. (See page 358 for the Taoist interpretation of the river, which concentrates less on unity and more on acceptance.)

The natural aim of a river is to flow to the sea, and this can be viewed as a metaphor for our deep need to connect with the spiritual source. The process of meditation has been likened to diving into an ocean of peace, with thoughts viewed as bubbles rising to the surface of the mind. If the sea suggests maturity and experience (infinite wisdom), at the opposite extreme from this is the spring (infinite energy). Meditating on a spring can help you to recapture the childlike, joyful aspect of yourself. A well, half-way in its symbolism between ocean and spring, signifies the wisdom of the unconscious that can rise, or be brought, to the surface and be used appropriately – although there is additionally a strong connotation of mystical healing.

ANIMAL NATURE

We can learn much about ourselves from animals. Although we consider ourselves to be special creatures, sitting comfortably at the top of the evolutionary scale, our basic instincts are no different from those of many other creatures with whom we share our planet. Like all animals, our primary urge is survival, both individually and as a species, and our need for the companionship of the opposite sex is specifically attuned toward fulfilling this drive. Animals are focused on living fully in the moment – something that sages constantly remind us to do in order to experience the richness of life. Our fellow creatures give all their attention to the needs of each moment, whether this is feeding, playing, reproducing or home-building, and are free from our purely human anxieties about the future. Features as varied as our opposing thumbs and our ability to imagine, and to write, set us apart from other creatures and have changed the face of the world, but it is important

to remember that *Homo sapiens* can be guided in many ways by other animals.

Every species embodies a quality that is recognizable within human nature. By observing an animal as a mandala in motion, an expression of the energy of the created cosmos, you can intuitively discover more about the various aspects of yourself, and this leads to an increased sense of wholeness. If you pay attention, you can discover much that is useful and inspiring even within a small garden or patch of earth.

Watching ants move in an orderly line to transport food back to the nest can teach you about cooperation, the spirit of working in harmony that brings sustenance to all. The shimmering wings of a dragonfly can be seen as a message to liberate yourself from the realm of illusion, and seek your own expression of who you truly are. Following the flight of a bird across the sky reminds you of the freedom of the spirit, and can enable your mind to soar to fresh heights of imagination and inspiration. The zigzag path of swallows, the effortless hovering of a bird of prey, and the perfect formation of a flight of geese as they track the Earth's magnetic field, can raise your spirits and enable you to find solutions to problems if you are feeling confined. The proud beauty of a peacock spreading its tail, and the tiny delicacy of a hummingbird, can remind you of the magnificent beauty within yourself as well as in the world around you.

The independence of a domestic cat is a reflection of the spirit of its larger wild cousins. Observing these creatures is a study in feline grace and strength, and can remind you that there is an inherent beauty in the ability to be comfortably alone with your thoughts.

The nobility of the large cats such as lions and tigers lies in their ability to create a balance between the qualities of power, strength and intent. Dogs, like their cousins the wolves, are fiercely loyal to those whom they consider to be kin, whether animal or human, and teach us about the power of faithfulness and constancy. Watch a school of dolphins and you will become immersed in a joyful sense of freedom and play, and can observe the spirit of cooperation in action. The ability of a snake to shed its skin is a message to leave the past behind and to embrace change.

Moths and butterflies teach us about transience. The life span of an adult moth is less than a week, sometimes only a few hours. Some species of moths do not have a mouth, as they do not live for long enough to feed. Their brief existence is taken up solely with the need to perpetuate the species. Butterflies are a symbol of transformation. From the simple egg through the larval phase, through the formation of the chrysalis to the emergence of the fragile winged insect, we can learn that humble beginnings can lead to great beauty.

If you view each creature that you encounter as one of nature's intricate mandalas, you will find that your respect for the complexity of ecological balance is increased, and you will be reminded of the many facets of yourself that can be brought to bear in any circumstance. If you have a question about the most appropriate way to deal with a situation, allow your mind to wander freely, and see which animal springs to mind. Its characteristic appearance or behaviour or its symbolic meaning may give you the answer you seek.

FLOWERS

Flowers universally suggest beauty, youth and gentleness, but in many cultures they can also symbolize innocence, peace, spirituality, the transience of life or the pure bliss of paradise. Denoting nature at its peak, they could be said to compress into one telling image the whole span of birth, life, death and rebirth.

Ikebana, the Japanese art of flower arranging, concentrates very much on this symbolic theme. It emphasizes shape, line and form, and tends to favour simple, even minimalist, arrangements, focused around three key points in a triangle. Practitioners of Ikebana treat their art as a form of meditation, always performed mindfully and in silence. It is often associated with Zen Buddhism.

In botany, *Compositae* is the term for one of the largest families of flowering plants, encompassing many thousands of

FLOWER WISDOM

Below is a directory of flowers with notes on their richest symbolic associations.

Anemone Transience, grief (Europe). The flower of Adonis, whom Venus transformed into an anemone.

Camellia Health and fortitude (China) – though linked with sudden death in Japan.

Chrysanthemum Sun and empire, longevity and happiness (Japan). In Chinese Taoist tradition, it is associated with perfection, tranquillity and abundance – the last of these related to the fact that the chrysanthemum blooms into winter.

Heliotrope or Sunflower Devotion (Europe) – because the flower head follows the sun. In China this flower was the food of immortality.

Lily Purity, virginity, piety (Christianity). The Archangel Gabriel held a lily when delivering the Annunciation to the Virgin Mary. The "lily of the fields" often mentioned in the Bible is actually an anemone.

Lotus The most important flower symbol of the East – it represents spiritual growth, birth and rebirth, and creation. In Hinduism the sacred lotus grew from the navel of Vishnu as he rested on the waters, giving birth to Brahma. Buddhist gods are often depicted sitting on a lotus.

Marigold Longevity (China); the god Krishna (India); the Virgin Mary (Christianity).

Narcissus Death, sleep, rebirth (Europe).

Pansy Loving remembrance (Europe). The name comes from the French pensée ("thought").

Peony The imperial flower of China. Associated with wealth, glory, nobility. Sometimes described in the West as "the rose without thorns".

Poppy Sleep, dreams, sacrifice (Europe).

Rose The white rose represents innocence, purity and virginity. The red rose symbolizes passion, desire and voluptuous beauty, as well as sacrifice (the thorns suggest suffering), martyrdom, death and resurrection.

Sunflower see **Heliotrope**.

species, including the numerous different daisies. A single daisy flowerhead contains around 250 separate flowers, with a core of 200 disk florets (often yellow) surrounded by 50 marginal ray florets (often white). The structure of a sunflower, another member of the *Compositae* family, is very similar. Any daisy-like flower has a concentric symmetry that offers us a wonderful natural mandala, because when you meditate on it you can discover many worlds within the single world of the individual flowerhead – making it a profound embodiment of the multi-layered nature of existence.

Flowers, of course, unlike insects, stay still when you want them to, which means that you can readily use them, inside or outside, to perform a mandala meditation. Their aptness for this purpose is increased by the traditional symbolism that underlies many flowers (see box, page 315). In Victorian times different flowers were given specific significance in a whole repertoire of encoded meanings related to courtship, friendship, marriage and mourning. More relevant to meditation, however, is the spiritual symbolism that certain flowers have carried for thousands of years. The lotus, which has its roots in the mud and its beautiful, pristine blossoms above the surface of a lake, has long been a symbol of enlightenment – of our ability to grow through the murky elements of the material self and express the beauty of the soul in our daily lives. The rose is unusual in having secular, romantic implications as well as equally powerful evocations of the spirit – two sets of meanings that intersect with each other in the ambiguities of the word "love".

Left: Roses tend to have an enfolded centre, which makes them appropriate for a multi-layered mandala meditation, somewhat akin to meditating on a spiral.

OUT OF THE ACORN

THE ACORN IS A PROVERBIAL SYMBOL OF POSSIBILITY: A CAPSULE
OF A FUTURE LIFE AS A MIGHTY OAK SMALL ENOUGH TO BE HELD IN THE
PALM OF THE HAND. OUR OWN POTENTIAL AS CREATIVE, NURTURING
SOULS MAY SIMILARLY OUTSTRIP ALL EXPECTATIONS.

1 Look at the acorn in the centre of the mandala: a mysterious rounded egg-like form that contains all developments to come encoded within it – rather like the future that is encoded in all the innumerable events of past and present.

2 Now turn your eyes to the fully grown tree, a parent of many acorns: the triumph of potential made actual.

3 Look next at the leaves surrounding the central square. So amazingly condensed is the acorn that every vein of every leaf of the adult tree is contained within the acorn's set of miniature biological instructions.

4 Finally, look at the circle within the square – spiritual perfection incarnated within the cosmos, like the mature oak tree incarnated within the acorn.

*"Start with what you know. Mature according
to nature. Let destiny do the rest."*

Zhuangzi (*c*.369–286 BC)

THE PATH OF LOVE

*"Pursue some path, however narrow and crooked,
in which you can walk with love and reverence."*

Henry David Thoreau (1817–1862)

THE SELF AS TREE

*"Like a tree I stand, reaching for the light,
gaining strength from the darkness at my roots.
My body is twisted by the storms of life,
yet in my uniqueness I am beautiful."*

Modern affirmation

THE DARK WOOD

THE MEDIEVAL ITALIAN POET DANTE BEGAN HIS *INFERNO* WITH
HIMSELF WALKING ALONE, LOST IN A DARK WOOD (*SELVA OSCURA*) —
SYMBOLIZING THE CONFUSIONS WE CAN EXPERIENCE IN OUR MIDDLE
YEARS. AFTER WRONG TURNS AND ENCOUNTERS WITH WILD BEASTS,
HE COMES ACROSS THE GHOST OF THE POET VIRGIL, WHO HAS COME
TO GUIDE HIM BACK TO HIS PATH, TO THE NEARBY MOUNTAINTOP.
VIRGIL SAYS THE ROUTE WILL TAKE THEM THROUGH HELL BUT THAT
EVENTUALLY THEY WILL REACH HEAVEN, WHERE DANTE'S BELOVED
BEATRICE AWAITS. IT WAS BEATRICE WHO, SEEING DANTE LOST, SENT
VIRGIL TO GUIDE HIM. APPLY THIS TALE TO YOUR OWN LIFE. JUST HOW
DENSE IS THE WOOD, AND HOW LOST ARE YOU? WHAT ARE THE WILD
BEASTS? WHO IS YOUR BEATRICE, WHO YOUR VIRGIL?

CHERRY BLOSSOM

THE BLOSSOM OF ANY FRUIT TREE TENDS TO CLING PRECARIOUSLY AND BEAUTIFULLY TO ITS BOUGH, THEN COMES A GUST OF BREEZE AND THE BLOSSOM TREMBLES AND FALLS TO THE GROUND. THE VERY TRANSIENCE OF BLOSSOM IS WHAT MAKES IT SO PRECIOUS.

1 Look at the square form in which the mandala sits – representing the solidity and density of the material world, as well as the constructs, mental and physical, by which we live our lives.

2 Contemplate the inner circle of the mandala, suggesting perfection and spirituality. While we live in this body, this perfection is accessible to us only by special privilege.

3 Hold the cherry blossom in your mind – it is one of many (represented by the eight smaller flowers) but is nonetheless worthy of your utmost concentration. Sense its beauty and its precariousness – its hold on the branch is uncertain.

4 Gaze into the heart of the flower. Here you see its transience and beauty coalesced into a single wonderful psalm of pure joy.

"In the cherry blossom's shade there is no such thing as a stranger."

Kobayashi Issa (1763–1827)

A RAIN OF BLOSSOM

"Untouchable pale petals, already saying goodbye.
Let us celebrate their parting while welcoming
the fresh spring breeze."

Anonymous modern haiku, Japan

NATURE'S WISDOM

"Study what the pine and cherry blossom can teach.
Man is not the only keeper of enlightenment."

Tao Te Ching (6th century BC)

CHERRY VIEWING

THE VIEWING OF CHERRY BLOSSOM, WHILE ENJOYING A PICNIC, HAS BEEN A TRADITIONAL CELEBRATION IN JAPAN FOR ALMOST TWO MILLENNIA. THE BLOSSOMS, WHICH LAST LESS THAN A WEEK, ARE A HARBINGER OF SPRING; BUT, OF COURSE, THEY ARE ALSO A POIGNANT REMINDER OF LIFE'S TRANSIENCE. THERE ARE SYMBOLIC LINKS WITH THE SAMURAI WARRIOR, WHO, LIKE BLOSSOM, OFTEN FELL AT THE HEIGHT OF GLORY. APPRECIATION OF FLEETING BEAUTIES IN NATURE CAN ENRICH EVERYONE'S YEAR. CONSIDER ARRANGING A PICNIC AROUND SOME NATURAL CLIMAX — FOR EXAMPLE, THE BRIEF, SPECTACULAR BLOOMING OF MAGNOLIA IN SUBURBAN GARDENS. SUCH AN EVENT ATTUNES YOU TO NATURAL CYCLES AND OPENS UP YOUR SENSES TO THE SMALL THINGS THAT MATTER.

THE RED ROSE

THE ROSE IS A MYSTICAL SYMBOL OF THE HEART. IN MANY TRADITIONS
THE RED ROSE ALSO DENOTES SACRIFICE, AS THE REDNESS CONJURES
UP AN IMAGE OF BLOOD, WHILE THE BEAUTY OF THE ENFOLDED PETALS
SUGGESTS THE LOVE THAT HAS INSPIRED SUCH SELFLESSNESS.

1 Look at the square and the equal-armed cross, whose elements represent the created cosmos. Surrounding this is the circle, a symbol of spiritual perfection.

2 Imagine the intersection of the cross behind the flower, suggesting the four cardinal directions and the incarnation of spirit in the material world. The cross supports the rose, whose flowering transcends it.

3 Gaze at the rose within its border of surrounding leaves. The flower is both our loss and our gain: in living our lives within nature's endless cycles, we experience the glorious flowering of the soul.

4 Lose yourself in the petals. The self is annihilated in the flowering of love within the heart. Take the rose into your inner self, and let it bloom in a burst of spiritual intensity.

*"Rose, we are your coronation ... the infinite
concordance of spirit unfolding."*

Rainer Maria Rilke (1875–1926)

NATURAL UNDERSTATEMENT

"One of the most attractive things about the flowers is their beautiful reserve."

Henry David Thoreau (1817–1862)

THE GIFT OF FRAGRANCE

"The world is a rose; smell it and pass it to your friends."

Persian proverb

THE ROSE OF LOVE

THE ROSE CAN BE A FERTILE SOURCE OF MEDITATIONS ON LOVE, THANKS
TO ITS TRIPLE SYMBOLISM — IT CAN DENOTE SACRED, ROMANTIC
AND SENSUAL LOVE. AND BECAUSE THE ROSE IS ALSO AN EMBLEM OF
PERFECTION, THERE IS A SUGGESTION THAT ALL THREE TYPES COHABIT
WITHIN THE ENLIGHTENED SELF, NAMELY: LOVE OF AND FOR THE
DIVINE; LOVE OF A SPECIAL PARTNER WITH WHOM ONE CHOOSES TO
MAKE A FUTURE; AND THE PHYSICAL LOVE BY WHICH THAT FUTURE IS
EXTENDED. ADD TO THESE THE LOVE OF ALL BEINGS IN THE COSMOS
AND THE TRIANGLE IS SQUARED. TRY THIS SIMPLE MEDITATION ON
WHOLENESS: IMAGINE A ROSE BOTH RED (WORLDLY) AND WHITE
(SPIRITUAL), THEN VISUALIZE THE TWO HUES FUSING TOGETHER, AS A
SYMBOL OF THE ADJUSTED SELF.

THE CHRYSANTHEMUM

IN CHINA THE CHRYSANTHEMUM IS THE EMBLEM OF TAOIST PERFECTION, AUTUMNAL SERENITY, FULLNESS AND LONGEVITY — BECAUSE ITS BLOOMS CONTINUE INTO THE WINTER. THE FLOWER IS ALSO A SOLAR SYMBOL, SAID TO SERVE AS AN INTERMEDIARY BETWEEN HEAVEN AND EARTH.

1 Look at the geometry of the mandala – the triangles and the circles. The large upward-pointing triangle is masculine and symbolizes fire; the large downward-pointing triangle is feminine and denotes water. The upper part of the upward triangle has the base of the downward triangle passing through it, denoting air; the lower part of the downward triangle also has a bar across it, denoting earth. Here are all the elements.

2 Now observe the central chrysanthemum – human ingenuity has bred this flower in many different hues, yet its natural essence remains intact, an independent being within the cosmos, subject to no human will.

3 Take this many-petalled radiance into your mind, and let it lie there as a reflection of your blossoming self, the flowering of being beyond becoming.

"Life is the flower for which love is the honey."

Victor Hugo (1802–1885)

A GARDEN WITHOUT WEEDS

*"Having realized his own self as the Self,
a person becomes selfless."*

Upanishads (*c.*1000 BC)

IN THE STILL DEPTHS

*"Like weary waves, thought flows upon thought,
but the still depth beneath is all thine own."*

George Macdonald (1824–1905)

FLOWERS OF THE SELF

FLOWERS HAVE INDESCRIBABLE SPLENDOUR. ROOTED IN EARTH, THEY STRIVE FOR LIGHT. THEY THRIVE BEST UNDER INFORMED, SYMPATHETIC CARE. ALL THESE CHARACTERISTICS MAKE THE FLOWER A SUITABLE IMAGE OF THE SELF, AND READILY AVAILABLE AS AN OBJECT FOR MEDITATION. IMAGINE A PARTICULAR FLOWER AS A CONCENTRATION OF YOUR OWN QUALITIES: FOR EXAMPLE, IF YOU SEEK TO NOURISH ACCEPTANCE WITHIN YOURSELF, THINK OF THE FLOWER ACCEPTING ALL WEATHERS — EVEN THE DROUGHT THAT MAKES IT THIRST AND THE CLOUDS THAT DEPRIVE IT OF SUNLIGHT. BY ABSORBING THIS IMAGE OF THE FLOWER, AND ITS SIMPLE INTERPRETATION, WE GIVE LIFE TO AN IDEAL OF THE SELF — AND FROM THE IMAGE SPRINGS AN ENERGY FOR POSITIVE CHANGE.

TWO TREES FROM ONE ROOT

NON-DUALISM IS THE BELIEF THAT, BEHIND NATURE'S DIFFERENCES, THERE
IS AN ESSENTIAL ONENESS. THESE TWO TRUNKS FROM ONE ROOT SHOW
DUALITY EMERGING FROM UNITY, YET REMAIN TRUE TO THEIR ONENESS IN
THE REALITY THAT UNDERLIES APPEARANCES.

1 Notice the contradictory perspectives in this mandala: there is no top, no bottom. The two trees inhabit a spiritual space rather than a physical space.

2 Start by looking at the four trees in the corners of the square image, outside the outer circle. This is differentiated nature. The trees belong to the same species but they are different trees, different lives.

3 Now look at the dance-like pattern of leaves within the broad brown circular band. We see the dance of nature and sense that its separate elements are connected.

4 Finally, look at the two trees joined at the roots. At the centre, where the roots are, is a *bindu* – an intense focus of energy. Lose yourself within this focus: as you do so, realize your oneness with the cosmos.

*"Wonder of wonders! This very enlightenment is the nature
of all beings, and yet they are unhappy for lack of it!"*

The Buddha (*c*.563–*c*.460 BC), at the moment of his awakening

WAYS OF SEEING

*"The tree which moves some to tears of joy is
in the eyes of others only a green thing that stands
in the way. Some see Nature all ridicule and deformity,
and some scarce see Nature at all. But to the eyes of the
man of imagination, Nature is Imagination itself."*

William Blake (1757–1827)

CIRCULAR MOTION

*"No matter how high the tree grows,
the leaves always return to the root."*

Malay proverb

THE INVERTED TREE

AMONG THE MOST POTENT OF TREE SYMBOLS IS THE INVERTED
TREE OF KABBALIST BELIEF AND PRACTICE — THAT IS, THE MYSTICAL
TRADITION WITHIN JUDAISM. THIS TREE HAS ITS ROOTS IN THE
SPIRITUAL REALM AND GROWS DOWNWARD TO THE EARTH. THE
IMAGE SYMBOLIZES THE CREATIVE POTENCY OF THE SPIRIT AS
WELL AS THE NOTION THAT OUR LIVES RESULT FROM THE DESCENT
OF SPIRITUAL ENERGY INTO BODILY FORM. SOME KABBALISTS
USE THE INVERTED TREE IN MEDITATION AS A SERIES OF STEPS BY
WHICH THEY ASCEND BACK TOWARD THE ROOT — THAT IS, TOWARD
DIVINITY, TO ACQUIRE A DIRECT EXPERIENCE OF GOD. THE INVERTED
TREE IS A LIVING EMBODIMENT OF THE MAIN KABBALIST IMAGE — THE
LADDER OF THE TEN *SEFIROT*, OR THE TEN ASPECTS OF GOD.

A WORLD OF LEAVES

FROM SUCCESS AND GOOD FORTUNE TO PILGRIMAGE AND DIVINITY,
THE LEAVES OF DIFFERENT TREES SYMBOLIZE MANY THINGS IN WORLD
CULTURES. ON A UNIVERSAL LEVEL, LEAVES CAN REPRESENT THE FLOWING
LIFE-FORCE OF NATURE, AND THE TURNING OF THE SEASONS.

1 Look at the central maple leaf – in ancient heraldry a single leaf signifies happiness. Red is the colour of fertility and energy. Feel that energy radiating through the leaf from its central stalk to its outer edges, which bound the leaf's completeness.

2 Now visually trace the veins of the leaf outward as they radiate into the leaves in the outer circle of the mandala.

This represents the individual leaf connecting with all the other leaves, and the larger organism they support and that supports them – the tree.

3 As you inhale and exhale slowly and deeply to sustain your meditation, harmonize your breathing with the leaves, as they "breathe" out oxygen into the surrounding air, thus sustaining the life of the tree, and the whole planet.

"And the leaves of the tree were for the healing of the nations."

Revelation 22:2

TREE AFTER WIND

"The poise of a plant, the bended tree recovering itself from the strong wind, the vital resources of every vegetable and animal, are also demonstrations of the self-sufficing, and therefore self-relying, soul. All history from the highest to its trivial passages is the various record of this power."

Ralph Waldo Emerson (1808–1882)

REST AMIDST CHANGE

"Praise and blame, gain and loss, pleasure and sorrow come and go like the wind. To be happy, rest like a great tree in the midst of them all."

Achaan Chaa (1918–1992)

LEAF LINES

HERE IS A SIMPLE VISUALIZATION TO BRING YOU CALM WHEN
WORRIES ARE NAGGING AWAY AT YOUR MIND. THINK OF A TREE IN AN
AUTUMNAL WIND, ALL THE BROWN AND RUSSET LEAVES THRASHING
AROUND, OFTEN TOUCHING EACH OTHER, AND SOME OF THEM FALLING
TO THE GROUND. THIS IS AN IMAGE OF YOUR MANY NIGGLING
ANXIETIES. BUT NOW IMAGINE THE WIND DROPPING, AND THE TREE
CANOPY GRADUALLY COMING TO STILLNESS, AND GETTING QUIETER
BY THE MINUTE. A FEW LEAVES ARE STILL FLUTTERING DOWN TO THE
GROUND, BUT THESE ARE THE VERY LAST. THE AIR IS NOW MOTIONLESS,
AND ALL IS CALM. IT IS NOW SO QUIET THAT YOU CAN HEAR BIRDSONG.
YOUR ANXIETIES HAVE FALLEN AWAY, LIKE THE LEAVES SHED BY THE
TREE. YOU ARE AT PEACE.

PAGODAS, POOL AND SKY

THIS MANDALA DEPARTS FROM THE TRADITIONAL ASSOCIATION OF GARDENS WITH GREENERY, INSTEAD DRAWING UPON JAPANESE IMAGERY AND THE SYMBOLISM OF RED AS THE LIFE-PRINCIPLE. PAGODAS ARE EMBLEMATIC MOUNTAINS, AND ALSO DENOTE THE LAYERS OF EARTH AND THE HEAVENS.

1 Look at the eight pagodas around the central pool. Their upper levels represent the heavens, echoed in the blue sky. Imagine also their foundations, deep in the earth – suggested by the fiery redness of the image.

2 Turn to the pool, with its surround of sky, clouds and birds. We are simultaneously looking down from an aerial perspective and up from an earth-bound perspective.

3 At the same time we can see the decorative motifs on the inside walls of the pagodas – so that we see both their outsides and their insides, breaking down our preconceptions.

4 Finally, look at the surface of the pool, where it meets the air – an interface between two elements. The circle between pool and sky is eternity. Pass through the circle into the garden of ultimate peace.

"The divine is there for all of us to see, reflected in the world's beauty, like clouds in the stillness of a lake."

Jonathan Borges (1872–1929)

PEONY IN A FIELD

CALLED THE "FLOWER OF TWENTY DAYS" ON ACCOUNT OF ITS
BRIEF FLOWERING SEASON, THE PEONY IS AN EASTERN SYMBOL OF
WEALTH AND PROSPERITY, BUT SHOWN AMIDST EARS OF GRAIN IT
DENOTES DOMESTIC JOY, A CONTENTED MARRIAGE AND FERTILITY.

1 Start by looking at the wheat or maize within the outer square border of this mandala. This is the domestic life we construct for ourselves by means of homes, domestic arrangements and provision of food.

2 Turn next to the four small peonies located in the corners of the square – perhaps these suggest the ideals of contentment that our society wishes us to strive toward.

3 Now contemplate the central peony of the mandala, flowering among the crop. Concentrate on the central core – which is also the core of the self, from which true joy flowers. Our responsibilities – to family, friends and society as a whole – form a framework to this intense experience of inner peace, and indeed to have one without the other would cause an imbalance, a sense of something missing.

"Love is infallible; it has not errors, for all errors are the want of love."

Andrew Bonar Law (1858–1923)

THE THORNLESS ROSE

THE PEONY HAS BEEN DESCRIBED AS A ROSE WITHOUT THORNS — SUGGESTING PERHAPS THE POSSIBILITY OF HAPPINESS WITHOUT SACRIFICE. THINK ABOUT THIS NOTION. ASK YOURSELF WHETHER TRUE HAPPINESS CAN BE POSSIBLE WITHOUT SOME KIND OF SELFLESSNESS OR SELF-DENIAL; OR PERHAPS IT IS SELFLESSNESS THAT MAKES THE THORNS DISAPPEAR? OR DOES THE SYMBOLISM BECOME MORE MEANINGFUL TO YOU IF THE ABSENCE OF THORNS IS ASSOCIATED WITH THE ABSENCE OF AGGRESSION OR DEFENSIVENESS? OR COULD THE IMAGE INSTEAD SUGGEST THE IDEA OF CONCEALING YOUR WOUNDS — THAT IS, NOT WEARING YOUR HEART ON YOUR SLEEVE FOR ALL TO SEE? PONDER AN IMAGINARY PEONY IN THIS WAY AND USE IT TO EXPLORE YOUR BELIEFS AND VALUES.

DESTINY'S CARPET

"Once we have found the true path, destiny unfolds itself like a carpet of glorious flowers."

Modern affirmation

BUD OR BLOSSOM?

"And the day came when the risk to remain tight in a bud was more painful than the risk it took to blossom."

Anaïs Nin (1903–1977)

THE LOTUS AND THE PINE

IN EASTERN SYMBOLISM THE LOTUS SUGGESTS ENLIGHTENMENT; THE OLD
PINE TREE, LONGEVITY OR OLD AGE. ENLIGHTENMENT CAN COME AT ANY
TIME. WHENEVER IT COMES, WE HAPPILY ACCEPT – EVEN EMBRACE – THE
INEVITABILITY OF AGEING AND OF THE BODY'S DECAY.

1 First, look at the gnarled pine trees around the circular frame of the mandala, and see them as a group of people who are your contemporaries in old age – everyone mellow and beautiful with antiquity.

2 Imagine moving from the clustered pine trees to the pond in the centre of the forest. This is where the lotus of enlightenment blooms with its roots in the mud – perhaps the mud is the reality of transience, the fact that all living things have their time.

3 Look at the beautiful lotus flower and see enlightenment blossoming in your mind, in the same way that the lotus petals have opened in their watery home. Feel the unfolding of petals inside your consciousness as you sit with your gaze still focused on the lotus.

*"Do not seek to follow in the footsteps of the
ancient ones; seek what they sought."*

Basho (1644–1694)

POET AMONG PINES

BASHO, WHO LIVED IN THE SEVENTEENTH CENTURY, IS JAPAN'S MOST CELEBRATED WRITER OF THE HAIKU, A FORM OF SHORT POEM THAT CAPTURES DEEP TRUTH IN AN OBSERVATION OF NATURE — NORMALLY WITH A SENSE OF GLORIOUS EVANESCENCE AS EACH MOMENT PASSES. BASHO WROTE JOURNALS, COMBINING PROSE AND POETRY, ABOUT LONG JOURNEYS THAT HE MADE ON FOOT THROUGH THE JAPANESE LANDSCAPE. START YOUR OWN NATURE DIARY, DESCRIBING YOUR WALKS IN THE COUNTRYSIDE, AND TRY INTERSPERSING YOUR PROSE DESCRIPTIONS WITH HAIKU THAT CAPTURE SPECIFIC OBSERVATIONS — SUCH AS A DRAGONFLY HOVERING OVER A STREAM OR THE FROST MELTING ON BARE BRANCHES. EACH HAIKU SHOULD HAVE ONLY THREE SHORT LINES. MAKE THE LANGUAGE AS DIRECT AS YOU CAN.

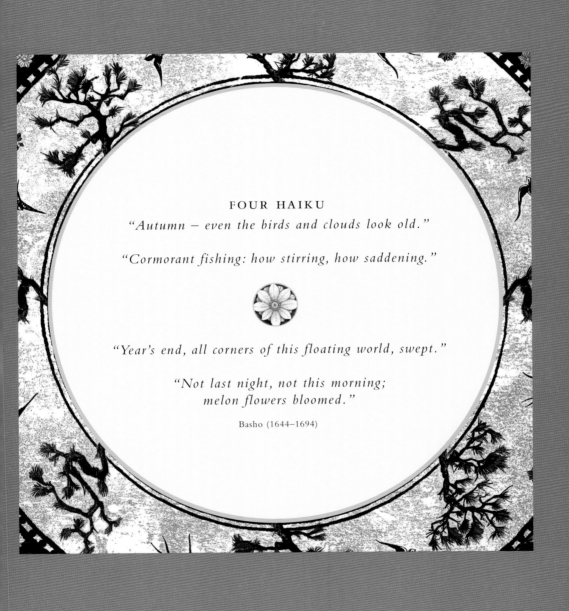

FOUR HAIKU

"Autumn — even the birds and clouds look old."

"Cormorant fishing: how stirring, how saddening."

"Year's end, all corners of this floating world, swept."

"Not last night, not this morning;
melon flowers bloomed."

Basho (1644–1694)

A Diamond's Light

ALL GEMSTONES BETOKEN LIFE AND CONSCIOUSNESS — LIGHT EMERGING
FROM THE DARK OF THE EARTH. INDIAN ALCHEMISTS REGARDED THE
DIAMOND AS THE ULTIMATE GOAL — IMMORTALITY. TANTRIC BUDDHISTS
SAW THE DIAMOND'S HARDNESS AS ANALAGOUS TO SPIRITUAL FORCE.

1 Start by contemplating the geometric framework of this mandala — the circle symbolizing eternity and the interlocking squares symbolizing the created world. All eight points of the two squares touch the circle — when eternity is glimpsed from within the prison of time, the prison walls dissolve.

2 Now look at the decorative framework within which the central diamond sits. Spiritual understanding requires a gracious setting of kind, loving thoughts and good, selfless actions.

3 Take the scintillating radiance of the diamond deep into your mind, and let it lie there as a reflection of your blossoming self, the flowering of being beyond becoming. Feel its spiritual force — the cutting edge of enlightenment.

"The created world is but a small parenthesis in eternity."

Thomas Browne (1605–1682)

A GARLAND OF FLOWERS

THE TRADITION OF USING FLOWERS TO CELEBRATE ACHIEVEMENTS OR
OCCASIONS BRINGS THE NATURAL WORLD TO OUR ATTENTION,
HINTS AT THE TEMPORARY STATUS OF ALL ENDEAVOUR OR SUCCESS,
AND HARNESSES NATURAL BEAUTY IN A FRAMEWORK OF ARTISTRY.

1 Look at the outer edges of the
mandala – a square, symbolizing
the created cosmos. Within the square
sits a succession of circles – symbolic
of spiritual perfection. Perhaps we
can attain enlightenment beyond the
confines of the physical?

2 Work inward toward the centre of
the mandala. As you do so, dwell on
each flower in turn and ask yourself
what its different characteristics might

symbolize; then find these qualities in
yourself. With successive stages of the
meditation, feel your insights becoming
deeper and deeper.

3 The garland celebrates your
success in moving to self-awareness.
Pause at the inner circle of decorative
embellishment. Beyond is a single
flower, with a deep yellow centre.
Pass beyond the world. Enter eternity.

*"The pursuit of truth and beauty is a sphere of activity
in which we are permitted to remain children all our lives."*

Albert Einstein (1879–1955)

DREAM WORLD

"The world is as you dream it."

Shamanic saying

MOUNTAIN REFUGE

"Climb the mountains and get their good tidings.
Nature's peace will flow into you as sunshine flows
into trees. The winds will blow their own
freshness into you ... while cares will drop
off like autumn leaves."

John Muir (1838–1914)

AN ALPINE FLOWER

CONJURE UP ALPINE FLOWERS IN A MEDITATION: IMAGINE YOURSELF
MAGICALLY TRANSPORTED TO A ROLLING GREEN MOUNTAIN
LANDSCAPE. ALL AROUND IS A PANORAMIC WILDERNESS. THERE
ARE CARPETS OF FLOWERS UNDERFOOT. YOU NOTICE WHITE BOG
ORCHID, SNOWBALL SAXIFRAGE, BRIGHT MAGENTA MOSS CAMPION,
AND ALPINE BUTTERCUPS. TAKE JUST ONE FLOWER YOU HAVE SEEN
SOMEWHERE AND VISUALIZE IT IN DETAIL. (REFRESH YOUR MEMORY
BEFOREHAND, IF YOU NEED TO, WITH A BOTANICAL FIELD GUIDE).
FEEL THE WIND IN YOUR HAIR AND ON YOUR FACE AND HANDS.
THINK OF THE FLOWER AS A PROUD, SELF-AWARE BEING — A LIVING
THING WITHOUT BLAME OR BLEMISH. LOOK WITHIN YOURSELF, AS IF
INTO A VAST LANDSCAPE, AND FIND THAT TINY FLOWER.

Flowing With The Stream

THE *TAO TE CHING* PLACES GREAT EMPHASIS ON THE INEVITABLE
FLOW OF NATURE — THE TAO ITSELF, IN WHICH WE MUST ALL
IMMERSE OURSELVES. THIS INVOLVES SURRENDERING ALL POINTLESS
RESISTANCE TO CHANGE AND ALLOWING NATURE TO TAKE ITS COURSE.

1 Look at this image of streams
meandering among rocks as if you were
looking down upon the scene from a
high mountain peak. You see the waters
swirling around great boulders as they
flow in different directions but are
inexorably bound toward the sea.

2 Think about which element — water
or rock — best expresses the essential
truth of human life. If we petrify to
become a boulder, we will endure.

If we dissolve into water, we will flow
and endlessly change, until one day we
reach the Source.

3 Trace the path of the four streams
outward across the rock-strewn
landscape. Where the waters crash
directly against a rock, there is
turbulence. Where the waters yield
and "step aside", there is movement —
which is the quintessence of life.

"If one way be better than another, that, you may be sure, is nature's way."

Aristotle (384–322 BC)

THE WORLD TREE

WITH ROOTS AROUND THE EARTH AND BRANCHES IN THE HEAVENS, THE
WORLD TREE IS A SYMBOL OF OUR ASCENT FROM THE PHYSICAL REALM TO
THE HIGHER LEVELS OF THE SPIRIT. THIS MANDALA OFFERS A PARADOXICAL
SPIN ON THIS IDEA BY HAVING THE EARTH'S CORE AS ITS CENTRAL POINT.

1 Look at the basic shape of the
mandala – a circle (symbolizing
eternity) within a square (symbolizing
the created cosmos).

2 Now turn your attention to the tree,
which connects our Earth with the
outer reaches of the universe – the
sun and moon are near neighbours of
ours, but the tree's branches stretch to
the very limits of eternity, unifying the
cosmos in their divine embrace.

3 Contemplate the Earth within
the tree's roots. The continent turned
toward you is Africa, where great
beauty and great poverty and suffering
coexist. Extend your love to all the
people in need upon this planet.

4 Let go of these imaginings and let
your mind penetrate right through to
the fiery core of the Earth, the deep
inner mystery at the heart of matter.
Lose yourself in this mystery.

*"The infinite has written its name on the heavens
in shining stars, and on Earth in tender flowers."*

Jean Paul Richter (1763–1825)

THE UNICORN

THE GREAT AUSTRIAN POET RAINER MARIA RILKE WROTE A SONNET
ABOUT THE UNICORN, BROUGHT INTO EXISTENCE BY OUR OWN BELIEF IN
IT. AS A GROUP OF VILLAGERS FED A HORSE WITH THEIR FAITH IN PURITY,
A HORN SPROUTED FROM ITS BROW. FAITH MAKES MIRACLES HAPPEN.

1 Look at the border of the mandala – a mixture of natural and man-made elements, like a garden. Our ideal existence on this Earth marries nature with civilization. The cultivation of beauty is akin to the cultivation of the soul.

2 Inside the circle's rim, white swallows fly – a glimpse of the miraculous, attainable to all of us who are open to wonder.

3 Now consider the rings within the tree-trunk, marking the passage of years. This is the nature we all live, the gift of our incarnation, fleeting but beautiful.

4 In a forest glade a white horse rears. We sense its strength, its natural perfection. By approaching the horse with selfless admiration, by believing in its purity, we win a priceless trophy: we glimpse the magic horn.

*"Beyond the pairs of opposites of which the
world consists, other, new insights begin."*

Hermann Hesse (1877–1962)

A QUESTION OF TIME

*"To every one of us there must come a time
when the whole universe will be found to have been
a dream, when we find the soul is infinitely better than
its surroundings. It is only a question of time, and time
is nothing in the infinite."*

Shirdi Sai Baba (1856–1918)

WHITE WISDOM

*"The milk of cows of any colour is white.
The sages declare that the milk is wisdom,
and that the cows are the sacred scriptures."*

Upanishads (*c.*1000 BC)

UNICORN QUEST

A UNICORN SUPPOSEDLY APPEARED TO THE EMPEROR HUANG DI
AS A TOKEN THAT HIS REIGN WOULD BE LONG AND PEACEFUL; AND
ANOTHER WAS THOUGHT TO HAVE BROUGHT A GIFT OF JADE TO THE
MOTHER OF CONFUCIUS AND LAID ITS HEAD ON HER LAP. EASTERN
UNICORNS SUGGEST GOOD OMEN. EVEN RICHER IS THE MEDIEVAL
CHRISTIAN TRADITION BY WHICH THE UNICORN REPRESENTS PURITY,
OR CONNECTION WITH THE DIVINE. ALTHOUGH A GENTLE CREATURE,
IT COULD USE ITS HORN DEFENSIVELY IF NEEDED. YOU CAN THEREFORE
INCLUDE THE CREATURE IN YOUR REFLECTIONS OR MEDITATIONS AS A
SYMBOL OF YOUR DESIRE TO BE CLOSER TO THE SPIRIT. ASK YOURSELF
WHAT THE HORN REPRESENTS. IN OTHER WORDS, WHAT PROTECTS
YOU FROM HARM AS YOU PURSUE YOUR QUEST FOR ENLIGHTENMENT?

GOLDEN APPLES

IN GREEK MYTH ONE OF THE TASKS UNDERTAKEN BY THE HERO HERAKLES, WAS TO TRAVEL TO A GARDEN WHERE TWO NYMPHS LIVED. THEY TENDED A TREE BEARING GOLDEN APPLES, GUARDED BY A MANY-HEADED SERPENT. IT WAS HERAKLES' TASK TO KILL THE SERPENT AND STEAL THE APPLES.

1 Imagine the orchard of the Hesperides, the two daughters of Atlas. One of the trees, depicted here, bears golden apples.

2 Trace a route to these apples, then start your journey, inward into the orchard and inward into the self, where all treasures lie.

3 Watching over the apple tree is a many-headed serpent – which you recognize to be an aspect of the self. The only truly dangerous enemies are those that lie within.

4 Look at the demon serpent and summon the qualities you need to banish this monster. You do not need to fight him – only to make him disappear by courageous resolve. Choose an apple from the tree and carry it deep into your inner self. This treasure is deservedly yours. What is it?

"The one chased away with a club comes back, but the one chased away with reason does not."

Kikuyu proverb, Kenya

THE SERPENT AND THE EGG

AN EGG SURROUNDED BY A COILED SERPENT WAS A POWERFUL SYMBOL IN
THE ANCIENT GREEK ORPHIC RELIGION, BUT ITS SYMBOLISM IS ESOTERIC.
NEVERTHELESS, THE UNIVERSAL SYMBOLISM OF THE EGG AND SERPENT
INDIVIDUALLY MAKES THIS IMAGE A REWARDING SUBJECT FOR A MANDALA.

1 Look at the four snake-encircled eggs – symbols of the cosmic serpent protecting the world. Sense the life-force flowing through the serpents. Their form suggests the spiralling motion of the cosmos. The egg is consciousness, protected by life itself.

2 Think of egg and serpent in terms of initiation. Enlightenment is the point at which spiritual practices break through the eggshell. This point is within our reach, but for now we keep both feet on the ground.

3 Contemplate the egg of consciousness intact within its powerful protection of faith. Its shell alone is not enough.

4 Look at the serpent eating its own tail – a celestial circle formed by the earth-bound creature. Rest your gaze on the central point.

*"A song slumbers in all things that lie dreaming on and on, and
the world prepares to sing, if you hit upon the magic word."*

Joseph Freiherr von Eichendorff (1788–1857)

LIFE-GIVING SUN

NOTHING IN OUR COSMOS CAN MATCH THE TRANSFORMATIVE POWER OF
THE SUN. IT EVEN PROVIDES US WITH THE MEANS TO SEE. DANGEROUS AT
FULL STRENGTH (LIKE THE GOD ZEUS, WHOM NO MORTAL COULD LOOK
UPON WITHOUT DYING), THE SUN IS ALSO PURE LIFE-GIVING ENERGY.

1 Contemplate the frame around the central image of the sun: an elegant pattern such as might be found in a sumptuous palace. Without the sun there would be no art, no civilization.

2 Focus on the central sun image: represented in traditional form as a disk with wavy rays. Understand as you absorb the image into your mind that the sun in its pure essence is beyond sensory experience (except as warmth and light) – in the same way that divinity cannot be comprehended at the sensory level.

3 Let your mind conjure the infinite energy of the sun as you contemplate its symbolic representation. Know that everything you feel derives from this incomprehensible source of love at the centre of our solar system.

*"The human body is vapour, materialized by
sunshine and mixed with the life of the stars."*

Paracelsus (1493–1541)

LOOKING INWARD

*"If the eye were not sun-like, it could not see the sun;
if we did not carry within us the very power of God,
how could anything God-like delight us?"*

Johann Wolfgang von Goethe (1749–1832)

COSMIC CREATION

*"That which has no form creates form. That which
has no existence brings things into existence."*

Rumi (1207–1273)

THE SOLAR SELF

WHENEVER WE NEED TO IMAGINE AN INFINITE SOURCE OF ENERGY,
OR BOUNDLESS QUALITIES OF ANY KIND, THE SUN PROVIDES US
WITH A PERFECT SYMBOL, EASY TO USE IN MEDITATION. FOR
EXAMPLE, WE MIGHT CHOOSE TO IMAGINE OURSELVES AS AN ENDLESS
SOURCE OF LOVE, SPREADING OVER ALL, BATHING FAMILY, FRIENDS,
ACQUAINTANCES AND STRANGERS ALIKE IN AN ALL-ENVELOPING
RADIANCE. NO OTHER PHENOMENON HAS SUCH CONNOTATIONS OF
INFINITE AND LIFE-GIVING ABUNDANCE. WE CAN "VISUALIZE" THE
SUN AS AN EXPLOSION OF LIGHT AND STRENGTH; AND WE HAVE
ONLY TO LOOK AROUND US, IN DAYLIGHT, TO OBSERVE HOW THE SUN
SPREADS ITS BENEFITS IN ALL DIRECTIONS. OUR OWN SPIRITUAL
ENERGIES, AND OUR CAPACITY FOR GIVING, ARE NO LESS IMPRESSIVE.

FROG OF GOOD FORTUNE

IN CHINESE FOLKLORE, THE THREE-LEGGED FROG WITH A COIN IN ITS
MOUTH IS AN AUGURY OF GOOD FORTUNE. ALTHOUGH TRADITIONALLY
ASSOCIATED WITH A MONETARY WINDFALL, THE CREATURE IN THIS
MEDITATION IS GIVEN A MORE SPIRITUAL DIMENSION.

1 Look at the magic frog – a strange creature that initially we might be inclined to find repellent, even if it were four-legged. Take a minute or so to accept the frog's disability as normal – banish any squeamishness from your mind.

2 Now start to think of the frog as your equal – a being with the right to existence, and to freedom from intolerance.

3 The frog could be eating flies, but instead it is making you an offering. You have no wish for money, but perhaps the coin is a symbol of something more meaningful – something your selflessness entitles you to?

4 See the coin as spiritual insight, which is self-rewarding. Focus your eyes on the coin's square centre. Take the coin into your mind, and be at peace.

*"I'm a great believer in luck, and I find
the harder I work the more I have of it."*

Thomas Jefferson (1743–1826)

JUST ONE SNOWFLAKE

NOTHING IS MORE LOVELY THAN THE DELICACY OF A SNOWFLAKE. IT
IS ONE OF NATURE'S FINEST ACHIEVEMENTS, NO LESS SO FOR THE FACT
THAT IT IS FLEETING. SIMILARLY, OUR BRIEF LIVES, AND EPISODES WITHIN
THEM, CAN BE BEAUTIFUL FOR ALL THEIR TRANSIENCE.

1 Look at this snowflake. It is complete
within itself, and totally unique, even
though it is one of millions in a
snow shower. Let the thought of the
snowflake's singular beauty sink into
your mind.

2 Now consider that this is an
artificial version of a snowflake, not a
real one. You are looking at an image,
because the reality of nature can be
captured only indistinctly, even when
we are out in the fields or woods
using all our senses.

3 Move to the centre of this abstract
pattern of a snowflake, and meditate
on it. Imagine a snow shower is falling
outside.

4 Absorb into yourself the yin-yang
symbol at the heart of the mandala –
the perfect balance of now and then,
now and eternity.

*"He who binds himself to a joy / Does the winged life destroy; /
But he who kisses the moment as it flies / Lives in eternity's sunrise."*

William Blake (1757–1827)

THE BEAUTY OF SNOW

WHEN SNOW FALLS ON A LANDSCAPE, WE OFTEN SEE ITS BEAUTY AFRESH. THE FAMILIAR BECOMES UNFAMILIAR. AND, OF COURSE, WE MAY FIND OURSELVES WALKING WHERE THERE ARE NO FOOTPRINTS, ENJOYING THAT LIBERATING FEELING OF BEING A PIONEER OF UNCHARTED TERRAIN. NEXT TIME YOU HAVE THE OPPORTUNITY TO GO FOR A WALK IN THE SNOW, TREAT IT AS A WALKING MEDITATION. IMAGINE THAT THE LANDSCAPE IS CHANGED, NOT BECAUSE IT LOOKS DIFFERENT, BUT BECAUSE YOU ARE DIFFERENT. FEEL IN YOURSELF A FRESHNESS OF SPIRIT, A RESTORED PURITY OR INNOCENCE, THAT IS SUITABLY SYMBOLIZED IN THE SNOW-CLAD LANDSCAPE. YOUR MISTAKES ARE ERASED, AND YOU NOW HAVE A BRAND-NEW PAGE, LIKE A FIELD OF SNOW, ON WHICH TO WRITE YOUR DESTINY.

FOOTPRINTS

"Do not go where the path may lead, go instead where there is no path and leave a trail."

Ralph Waldo Emerson (1803–1882)

MEETING THE MORNING

"Each soul must meet the morning sun, the new, sweet earth, and the Great Silence alone!"

Ohiyesa (1858–1939)

TRANSFORMING FIRE

FIRE SYMBOLIZES BOTH CREATIVE AND DESTRUCTIVE ENERGIES. IT CAN
SUGGEST PURIFICATION, REGENERATION, OR REVELATION — AS IN THE
BURNING BUSH WITNESSED BY MOSES. THIS MEDITATION PROGRESSES
FROM THE FLAME OF PURIFICATION TO THE FLAME OF INSIGHT.

1 Around the outer circle of the mandala is a ring of small fires you need to pass through to start your meditation. These are the purifying flames you need to bring to emotional attachments to burn them away.

2 The middle ring of bonfires may be seen as a welcome — a celebration that you have purified yourself. Yet there is further work to do, as you must access selflessness. At the deepest level

you must be prepared to give love and selfless service. This requires the burning of the ego.

3 Finally you pass into the heart of the mandala — God's "holy fire", as W.B. Yeats called it in his poem "Sailing to Byzantium". You feel an intense heat that does not burn, but rather enlightens — like a great lantern of infinite intensity. You are at peace.

"For indeed our God is a consuming fire."

Hebrews 12:29

THE PHOENIX

THE PHOENIX IS A LEGENDARY MALE BIRD WITH A BLAZE OF GLORIOUS GOLD AND RED PLUMAGE. AFTER LIVING FOR FIVE CENTURIES, IT WOULD BUILD A NEST FOR ITSELF OUT OF CINNAMON TWIGS, IGNITE THE NEST, AND THUS BURN ITSELF TO A PILE OF ASHES — OUT OF WHICH A NEW, YOUNG PHOENIX WOULD EMERGE. THE NEW PHOENIX WOULD THEN DEPOSIT THE REMAINS (EMBALMED IN A CASING OF MYRRH) IN HELIOPOLIS, THE CITY OF THE SUN. THE PHOENIX LATER BECAME A SYMBOL OF RESURRECTION. DWELL ON THIS SYMBOLISM WHENEVER YOU SEEK TO MAKE A DRAMATIC CHANGE IN YOUR LIFE. THINK OF YOURSELF AS THE YOUNG PHOENIX, BORN OUT OF THE DESTRUCTION OF BAD HABITS. IMAGINE THE FIRE FROM WHICH YOUR NEW SELF ARISES AS SIMULTANEOUSLY PURIFYING AND CREATIVE.

THE ESSENTIAL FLAME

"Just as a candle cannot burn without fire,
men cannot live without a spiritual life."

The Buddha (*c*.563–*c*.460 BC)

CALL OF THE PHOENIX

"O joy! that in our embers
Is something that doth live."

William Wordsworth (1770–1850)

SEASHELLS

AS WELL AS BEING AN AUSPICIOUS LUNAR, FEMININE EMBLEM ASSOCIATED
IN SOME CULTURES WITH FERTILITY AND GOOD FORTUNE, THE SHELL IN
ITS OFTEN COMPLEX INNER GEOMETRY REFLECTS THE MYSTERIOUS DIVINE
ORDER THAT UNDERPINS ALL CREATION.

1 Hold in your mind the border of sea and sand. Think of the waves endlessly breaking and reforming, like the cycles of time itself. Think also of the beach, furrowed by a retreating tide – in the same way, we are marked by the passage of years, while retaining traces of the spirit.

2 Contemplate the long, pointed shells shown in cross-section – without their inner geometry, these shells could not inhabit their own elegant form.

3 Finally, look at the beautiful double shell in the middle of the mandala. Think of the two spiralling globes as the complementary yin and yang – female and male, stillness and action, compassion and insight. Follow the spirals inward toward the ineffable source of creation, beyond the visible.

"Nature never says one thing and wisdom another."

Juvenal (late 1st/early 2nd century AD)

SEASHORE AND SPIRIT

SIR ISAAC NEWTON ONCE LIKENED HIMSELF TO A BOY PLAYING ON THE SEASHORE, DIVERTING HIMSELF BY FINDING A SMOOTHER PEBBLE OR A PRETTIER SHELL THAN USUAL, WHILE THE "GREAT OCEAN OF TRUTH" LAY UNDISCOVERED BEFORE HIM. THIS IMAGE CAPTURES OUR INABILITY TO FULLY COMPREHEND THE WONDER OF CREATION AND OF OUR OWN EXISTENCE. WE CAN APPRECIATE THE UNSEEN VASTNESS OF THE OCEAN ONLY BY EXTRAPOLATING FROM WHAT WE DO SEE — THE LINE WHERE SEA MEETS SKY. TO INTUIT THE SPIRIT WE MUST START WITH AN AWARENESS OF HOW INADEQUATE EVEN OUR HIGHEST FACULTIES ARE TO RECEIVE ANYTHING BUT A DIM APPROXIMATION. ONLY THEN CAN WE START TO ACQUIRE WISDOM.

THE LOGIC OF PARADISE

*"Sand, sea and sky — a progression toward
the sublime. Inwardly, unconsciously,
we complete the series: heaven."*

Louise Soustelle (1911–1962)

THE OCEAN OF TRUTH

*"If you would swim on the bosom
of the ocean of Truth, you must reduce
yourself to a zero."*

Mahatma Gandhi (1869–1948)

THE COILED SNAKE

THE MOST COMPLEX OF ANIMAL SYMBOLS, THE SNAKE HAS BEEN LINKED
VARIOUSLY WITH FERTILITY, HEALING AND DUPLICITY. ITS POWER TO
RENEW ITSELF BY SHEDDING ITS SKIN SUGGESTS REJUVENATION, AND IN
SOME EASTERN CULTURES IT IS LINKED WITH THE CREATOR DEITY.

1 Start by looking at the spirals and yin-yang symbols around the edge of the mandala. These denote the rhythms of life, the spiralling motion of the cosmos.

2 Turn to the snake, an image of the life-force, latent with regenerative energy – contrasting with the paved stonework it rests on. Also, the snake is the Other, an intelligence unknowable by the modern mind.

3 Dwell now upon the snake's coiled form. Follow the coil of the body from tail to head, and feel the intensity of its power increasing as you move toward the snake's brain.

4 From the head move your eyes to the ruby, glowing red, around which the snake is coiled. This is the mysterious gift of life itself, a benevolent enigma. Take this truth deep into your mind and relax within its power.

*"Snakes are the ambassadors of raw nature,
singing songs of mud and fire too solid for the ear."*

Pedro de Hermanandez (1920–2000)

THE ELUSIVE SNAKE

SNAKES DART FROM SHADOWS INTO SUNLIGHT AND BACK — A MYSTERIOUS FLASH OF PRIMEVAL LIFE, MAKING US AWARE OF A PRIMITIVE FORCE BEYOND CONSCIOUSNESS. DO THIS SIMPLE RAINFOREST MEDITATION TO CONNECT YOURSELF WITH THESE ENERGIES. SIT COMFORTABLY, CLOSE YOUR EYES AND IMAGINE THAT YOU ARE IN A VAST FOREST. IT IS DAYTIME BUT THE FOREST IS SO DEEP THAT NO LIGHT PENETRATES HERE. IMAGINE YOU ARE A TREE, YOUR LEAVES TOUCH THOSE OF THE TREES AROUND YOU. WITH YOUR INNER EYE YOU SENSE A SNAKE AMONG YOUR BRANCHES — BUT YOU DO NOT FEEL IT BECAUSE TOUCH IS FELT THROUGH YOUR LEAVES, NOT YOUR BARK. YOU INTUIT IT AS AN ELEMENT OF THE PRIMORDIAL WITHIN YOURSELF. AND YOU SENSE ITS HIDDEN POWER.

BEYOND THE SENSES

"Our eyes believe themselves, our ears believe other people, our intuition believes the truth of the spirit."

(adapted from a German proverb)

THE IMPACT OF NATURE

"When one withdraws all desires as a tortoise withdraws its limbs, then the natural splendour of the world soon manifests itself."

The Mahabharata (c.400 BC–c.AD 200)

FREEING THE WILD SWAN

THE CHAINED SWAN SUGGESTS POWER UNDER THE SUBJUGATION OF REASON — A TRAVESTY OF WHAT IT MEANS TO BE WILD. IN THIS MEDITATION WE AIM TO RELEASE THE BIRD INTO ITS TRUE ELEMENT, AT THE SAME TIME AS WE RELEASE OUR SPIRIT FROM ITS CONFINING BONDS.

1 Gaze on the feathers within the outer border of this mandala — tokens of the possibility of flight, and reminders that earth is not the only element in which we can live.

2 Now move inward to the two concentric bracelets of interlocking chains. These represent the human world — the imposition of order onto nature. And they also denote the price we pay for such control. Perhaps our dominance over nature can chain our own souls and prevent them from flight.

3 Look at the swan, tamed by humanity. Focus on the radiance of its white-feathered body — infinitely more dazzling than the gold necklace. Imagine that love is pouring from your heart into the creature's wounded soul. In your loving imagination you can release the swan to fly to freedom.

"When the swan of the soul takes flight at last, it needs neither signposts nor maps."

Vijay Bhattacharya (1879–1950)

SWAN SONG

ON ACCOUNT OF ITS DAZZLING WHITE PLUMAGE, THE SWAN
SYMBOLIZES LIGHT IN MANY OF THE WORLD'S CULTURES. IT HAS
SOMETHING OF A HERMAPHRODITE NATURE — SUGGESTING MASCULINE
POWER AS WELL AS FEMININE GRACEFULNESS AND INTUITION. THESE
TWO QUALITIES COMBINE IN THE GERMANIC MYTH OF THE VALKYRIE
(WARRIOR GODDESS) NAMED KARA. CONCERNED TO PROTECT HER
WARRIOR-LOVER HELGI DURING A BATTLE, KARA FLEW OVER THE
FIGHTING IN HER SWAN'S PLUMAGE AND SANG A SONG SO SUBLIMELY
SOOTHING, LIKE A LULLABY, THAT THE ENEMY ENTIRELY LOST THEIR
WILL TO FIGHT. IN ITS COMBINATION OF STRENGTH AND PURITY,
THE SWAN IS NOT UNLIKE THE UNICORN, AND THE CREATURE CAN BE
INCORPORATED INTO YOUR MEDITATIONS IN A SIMILAR WAY.

ASSUMED IDENTITY

*"I will cease to live as a self and will take as
my self my fellow-creatures."*

Shantiveda (*c*.7th century)

LOVE'S WINGS

*"The way to heaven is within. Shake the wings of
love — when love's wings have become strong,
there is no need to trouble about a ladder."*

Jalil al-Din Rumi (1207–1273)

WANDERING TERNS

THE ARCTIC TERN IS FAMED FOR ITS PRODIGIOUS MIGRATION, SUMMERING IN THE ARCTIC AND WINTERING IN THE ANTARCTIC TO GIVE ITSELF MAXIMUM DAYLIGHT. THIS MANDALA FOCUSES ON THE IDEA THAT MOBILITY, AS OPPOSED TO A RIGID NATURE, IS A POSITIVE QUALITY.

1 See the planet Earth at the centre of this mandala as an image of your imagination – a whole world that not even a lifetime's exploration could exhaust. Look beyond the Earth to layers of sky; and then beyond the outer circle of the cosmos, to an unimaginable blankness.

2 Now contemplate the terns on their long-distance migration from pole to pole. Your own imagination can travel even further. It can fly beyond the Earth up through layers of sky and cloud. It can imagine right up to the limits of the unimaginable.

3 Return your concentration to the Earth, and indeed to one spot on the globe in the centre of the mandala. Here, in one village, one house, one mind even, is a whole cosmos of richness and value. Just imagine.

"Imagination is everything. It is the preview of life's coming attractions ..."

Albert Einstein (1879–1955)

AMONG THE DOVES

THERE ARE VARIOUS WAYS IN WHICH YOU CAN USE BIRDS IN
MEDITATIONS OR IMAGINATIVE EXERCISES. FOR EXAMPLE, IF YOU
EVER FEEL THAT WORK, OR HOUSEHOLD CHORES, OR FAMILY
PRESSURES, HAVE BECOME SOMETHING OF A TREADMILL, YOU COULD
VISUALIZE YOURSELF AS A BIRD FLYING HIGH ABOVE THE LANDSCAPE,
LOOKING DOWN UPON YOUR LIFE IN THE OVERALL CONTEXT OF
YOUR COMMUNITY. TO REVITALIZE YOUR SENSE OF PURPOSE, YOU
MIGHT ENVISAGE THE POSITIVE IMPACT YOUR EFFORTS HAVE ON
THOSE AROUND YOU. OR ALTERNATIVELY YOU COULD CREATE A
VISUALIZATION AROUND THE IMAGE OF THE DOVE, OR THAT OF THE
HAWK. YOU MIGHT CHOOSE TO NURTURE ONE OR MORE OF THE
QUALITIES THAT THESE BIRDS REPRESENT.

PERFECT PRAYER

"One single grateful thought raised to heaven is the most perfect prayer."

G.E. Lessing (1729–1781)

ROOTS AND WINGS

"There are only two lasting benefits we can hope to give to our children. One is roots; the other, wings."

Hodding Carter (1907–1972)

A GOLDEN CARP

IN THE EAST THE CARP IS AN OMEN OF GOOD FORTUNE,
ESPECIALLY LONG LIFE, ON ACCOUNT OF THE FISH'S OWN LONGEVITY.
IT WAS ALSO GIVEN IN EMBLEMATIC FORM TO STUDENTS WITH WISHES
FOR SUCCESS IN EXAMINATIONS. THE CARP IN ITS POND CAN BE
LIKENED TO INSIGHT — A DISTINCT GLEAM IN THE MURKY DEPTHS.

1 Look at the overhead view of the pond represented in this mandala. Start with the raked gravel surround, symbolizing the flow of time. Then move to the pond's edge which takes the form of a circle, denoting our yearning for a glimpse of spiritual perfection, of eternity.

2 Gaze at the various living things in and around the pond: the butterflies, dragonflies and waterlilies. Look too at the fallen leaves, which remind us of the inevitability of decay in nature's cycle.

3 Pick out the subtle gleam of the carp, just visible in the inky waters. This may be our own good fortune, which habitual preoccupations often prevent us from seeing. Perhaps the carp is a dawning insight — a gratefulness that we are part of nature.

*"The eye of the silent heart will see into great depths,
and the ear of the silent mind will hear untold wonders."*

St Hesychius of Jerusalem (5th century AD)

SCALLOP SHELLS

LIKE OTHER KINDS OF SHELL, THE SCALLOP DENOTES FERTILITY AND
FEMININITY, THANKS TO ITS ASSOCIATION WITH WATER.
THE FACT THAT OYSTERS CONTAIN PEARLS GAVE RISE TO THE MYTH
OF APHRODITE BEING BORN OUT OF A SHELL.

1 Look at the wave forms within the circle that immediately surrounds the central scallop shell. Think of the ocean rising and falling in its tidal rhythms determined by the moon, symbol of eternal change.

2 Turn your attention to the outer circle of scallops framing the larger, central shell. Think of nature producing near-identical forms from the genetic blueprint of a species. The self is central, but in fact there are countless selves, all participating in the unified cosmos.

3 Move in your mind through the successive circles of the image, dwelling on each circular band in turn. Finally, let your eye rest on the central shell – the perfect moment within its framework of endless change.

"Peace is the one-way flow of time without any ripple of regret or resistance."
Marie le Strange (1890–1976)

THE PILGRIM'S PATH

*"Life can only be understood backwards;
but it must be lived forwards."*

Søren Kierkegaard (1813–1855)

WAY BACK

*"Reverse time's arrow and make it your signpost.
Revisit your old haunts and feel the years wither
and drop from your limbs, heart and brain."*

Samuel Haroldson (1912–1990)

THE PILGRIM SALMON

IN MEDIEVAL EUROPE THE SCALLOP SHELL WAS THE BADGE OF PILGRIMS. IN THE ANIMAL WORLD THERE IS NO MORE IMPRESSIVE PILGRIM THAN THE ATLANTIC SALMON, WHICH REACHES MATURITY IN THE OCEAN AND THEN TRAVELS THOUSANDS OF MILES TO THE UP-RIVER STREAMS WHERE IT FIRST SAW THE LIGHT OF DAY, ITSELF TO SPAWN. THE IDEA OF RETRACING OUR STEPS TO A PLACE OF ORIGIN IS AN APPEALING ONE. YOU MIGHT CONSIDER CONSTRUCTING A MEDITATION ON THIS IDEA — FOR EXAMPLE, ONE THAT TAKES YOU BACK TO A PHASE IN YOUR LIFE WHEN YOU FELT ESPECIALLY HAPPY, AND INVOLVES BRINGING SOME IMAGE OR VISUALIZED OBJECT BACK WITH YOU FROM THAT PERIOD, LIKE A TIME TRAVELLER; AND THEN USING THIS AS A TOTEM TO RENEW YOUR ENERGIES OR YOUR RESOLVE.

GAZING AT THE TIGER

WE MAY BE AT A LOSS TO UNDERSTAND THE MENTALITY OF SOMEONE WHO SPEAKS A DIFFERENT LANGUAGE FROM OUR OWN, YET AN ANIMAL'S CONSCIOUSNESS IS EVEN MORE BAFFLING. THIS PUZZLEMENT SHADES INTO AWE, WHICH, DEPRIVED OF ANY FEAR, BRINGS INSIGHTS.

1 With your eyes move slowly from the outer edge of the mandala toward the centre. Imagine first that you are entering the jungle, then a reserve within that jungle where wild tigers roam. You see four of them from a safe distance; and closer to the heart of the reserve you see four tiger footprints.

2 Now prepare for a closer encounter with a tiger by meditating on the Greek cross within a circle within a square – a miniature mandala in itself, suggestive of spirit (circle), the natural world (square), and the incarnation of spirit in creation (cross).

3 You are now given the privilege to come close to the tiger and look right into its eye. You lose yourself in its mystery, safe in the knowledge that your spiritual awareness protects you from any real danger.

"Humankind differs from the animals only by a little, and most people throw that away."

Confucius (551–479 BC)

A Bird's Egg

THE EGG IS A UNIVERSAL SYMBOL OF BEGINNINGS, WHOSE
FRAGILITY EMPHASIZES HOW PRECIOUS IT IS. AS WITH MANY
DIFFERENT KINDS OF PROJECT, CONDITIONS MUST BE RIGHT FOR
THE BREAKTHROUGH TO TAKE PLACE.

1 Look at the border around the egg, with its delicate leaves. These symbolize the preparation that any serious project of self-fulfilment or self-analysis, or any major new direction in life, requires. Trace the interwoven lines of the border as a symbolic gesture of readiness to acquire fresh insights.

2 Progress now to the egg itself, sitting on its intricately woven nest. Sense within the shell the new life pulsing with potential. Send out love from your heart to wrap the egg in a force-field of nurturing warmth.

3 Think for a moment of the change you would like to see – whether in yourself, or your family or friends, or your community. Bring the image of the egg deep into your consciousness, and imagine it getting ready to hatch. Finally, it does so. There is new life.

"Everything in nature contains all the power of nature.
Everything is made of one hidden stuff."

Ralph Waldo Emerson (1803–1882)

LIFE CYCLES

ANY ANIMAL WHOSE LIFE CYCLE HAS DISTINCT STAGES — A BIRD, A
BUTTERFLY, A FROG — MAY BE USED AS A TEMPLATE FOR MEDITATION
TO PREPARE YOURSELF FOR A LIFE CHANGE OF SOME KIND, AS
DESCRIBED ON PAGE 409. BIRDS HAVE THREE DISTINCT STAGES: THE
EGG; THE JUVENILE, WHICH MUST LEARN TO FLY AND FEED ITSELF;
AND THE ADULT, WHICH MAY OR MAY NOT MIGRATE. THE BUTTERFLY
IS A USEFUL IMAGE BECAUSE THE EMERGENCE OF THE ADULT FROM THE
CHRYSALIS IS BEAUTIFUL AND ENABLING. YOU COULD ALSO MEDITATE
AROUND A FROG'S LIFE CYCLE, BECAUSE A CREATURE CONFINED TO
WATER (THE TADPOLE) ACQUIRES THE ABILITY TO MOVE ON LAND.
WHICH OF THESE CREATURES YOU BUILD INTO YOUR MEDITATIONS IS
ENTIRELY, OF COURSE, A MATTER OF PERSONAL PREFERENCE.

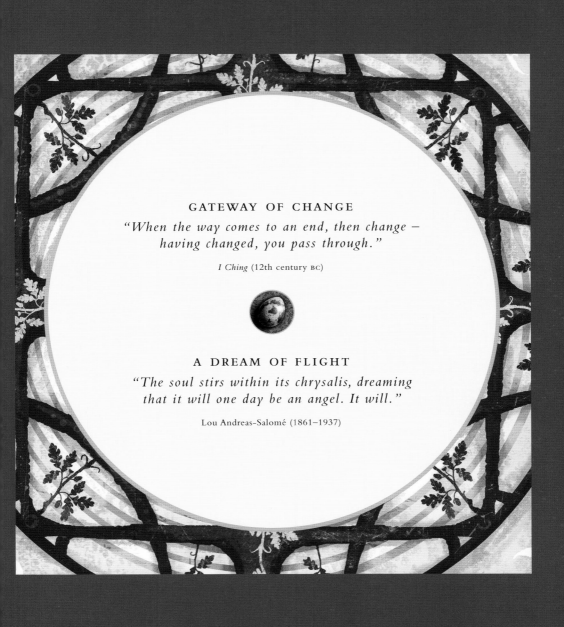

GATEWAY OF CHANGE

*"When the way comes to an end, then change —
having changed, you pass through."*

I Ching (12th century BC)

A DREAM OF FLIGHT

*"The soul stirs within its chrysalis, dreaming
that it will one day be an angel. It will."*

Lou Andreas-Salomé (1861–1937)

THE BUSINESS OF BEES

THE BEEHIVE IS AN IMAGE OF COOPERATIVE ENDEAVOUR
WITHIN A SOCIETY. THIS IDEA IS ENRICHED BY A SPIRITUAL
SYMBOLISM ATTACHED TO THE INDIVIDUAL BEE, IN ITS CONVERSION
OF NECTAR TO HONEY.

1 Look at the two concentric circles, symbolizing spirituality, and the square between them, denoting the created cosmos, which is also suggested by the various flowers.

2 Let your eyes rest in turn on the eight bees within the outer circle. Bees are emblematic of the soul, and hence participate in the spirituality that both circles of the mandala represent.

3 Pass into the inner circle (the hive, with its honeycomb), and rest your eyes on one of the bees that has filled the comb with honey. Think of the comb as your mind, and the honey as your awareness of the divine.

4 Take the mandala as a whole deep into your mind. Let the image of the hive fill your consciousness. Feel connected to the world community of the spirit.

"No one drop of honey can claim to be from the nectar of a single flower. All creatures are one but do not realize this."

Upanishads (*c.*1000 BC)

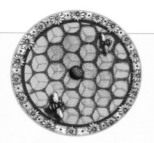

THE WORRY HIVE

THE IMAGE OF THE BEEHIVE CAN BE USED IN A VERY STRAIGHTFORWARD VISUALIZATION TO REDUCE LEVELS OF EVERYDAY STRESS. IF YOU ARE TROUBLED BY A CONSTANT BACKGROUND NOISE OF VAGUE ANXIETY, THEN FIND A QUIET PLACE TO SIT, CLOSE YOUR EYES, TAKE A FEW DEEP BREATHS AND START TO ENVISAGE ALL YOUR PROBLEMS AS A SWARM OF BEES BUZZING AROUND YOUR HEAD. IN YOUR MIND'S EYE CONJURE UP A BEEHIVE JUST IN FRONT OF YOU. THEN MENTALLY GUIDE THE BEES ONE BY ONE SAFELY INTO THE HIVE. WITH EACH BEE THAT IS BROUGHT HOME, THE BUZZING BECOMES A LITTLE QUIETER, UNTIL IT FINALLY CEASES ALTOGETHER. YOUR ANXIETIES — EVEN THE ONES THAT ARE NAMELESS — HAVE BEEN SHEPHERDED AWAY TO A PLACE WHERE THEY CANNOT CAUSE YOU ANY TROUBLE.

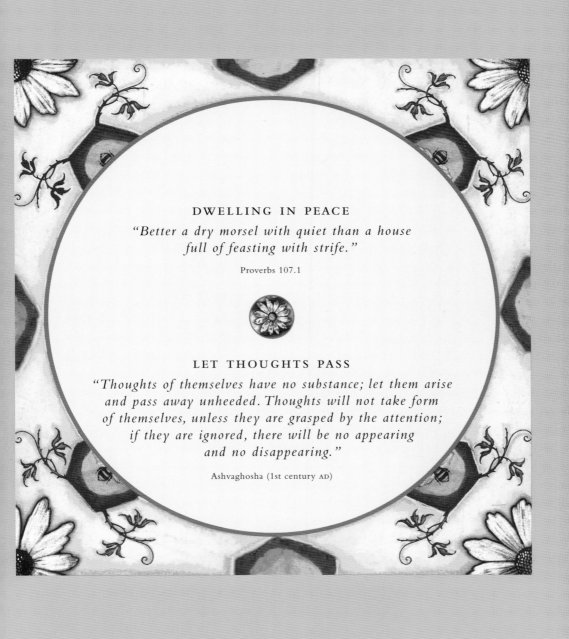

DWELLING IN PEACE

*"Better a dry morsel with quiet than a house
full of feasting with strife."*

Proverbs 107.1

LET THOUGHTS PASS

*"Thoughts of themselves have no substance; let them arise
and pass away unheeded. Thoughts will not take form
of themselves, unless they are grasped by the attention;
if they are ignored, there will be no appearing
and no disappearing."*

Ashvaghosha (1st century AD)

EYES OF THE PEACOCK

THE COSMOS HAS AN INTRINSIC RADIANCE THAT IS NOT ALWAYS
APPARENT: WE CAN BE DISTRACTED FROM BEAUTY AND WONDER BY OUR
EVERYDAY PREOCCUPATIONS. THE PEACOCK IS AN IMAGE OF REVELATION,
USED IN THIS MANDALA TO OPEN THE EYELID OF AWARENESS.

1 Start by looking at the outer circle of the mandala – symbol of eternity or spirit. Along the circumference are iridescent "eye" motifs of a peacock's tail. Could these have some connection, in their beauty, with the eternal?

2 Contemplate each concentric band of the mandala in turn. Dwell on the miracle of colour and pattern, and the vision that allows us so to perceive it so vividly.

3 Now gaze at the triangle within the mandala – a symbol of both harmony and, in alchemy, fire. Feather and fire coexist in a harmonious universe.

4 Lastly, dwell on the peacock itself. Life is beautifully, pricelessly evanescent, like the flash of a peacock's tail. Its perfection may be hidden, but the enlightened soul will see this glory – a wonderful gift from the One.

*"Dive deep, O mind, in the ocean of God's beauty! If you descend
to the utmost depths, there you will find the gem of love."*

Bengali hymn

OTHER MANDALAS

THE FOLLOWING COLLECTION OF 38 MANDALA DESIGNS ILLUSTRATES
SOME FURTHER EXCITING POSSIBILITIES THAT CAN OPEN UP WHEN
THE MANDALA IS FREED OF ITS MORE TRADITIONAL SYMBOLIC
ASSOCIATIONS AND IMAGERY. THE EXAMPLES IN THIS CHAPTER RANGE
FROM KALEIDOSCOPIC, CONCENTRIC PATTERNS TO PURE GEOMETRIC
FORMS, AS WELL AS NATURALLY OCCURRING PLANT AND ANIMAL
FEATURES. HERE AND THERE YOU WILL SEE VISUAL ALLUSIONS — TO
STAINED GLASS DESIGN, EASTERN MOTIFS, THE MIDDLE EASTERN
CARPET TRADITION, AND EVEN MEDIEVAL TAPESTRIES; AND, AT A
MORE DETAILED LEVEL, TO NATURE'S ABUNDANCE IN THE FORM OF
FLOWERS AND LEAVES.

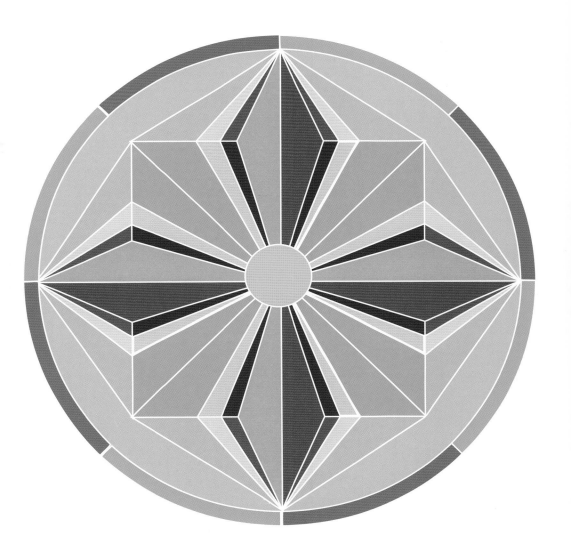

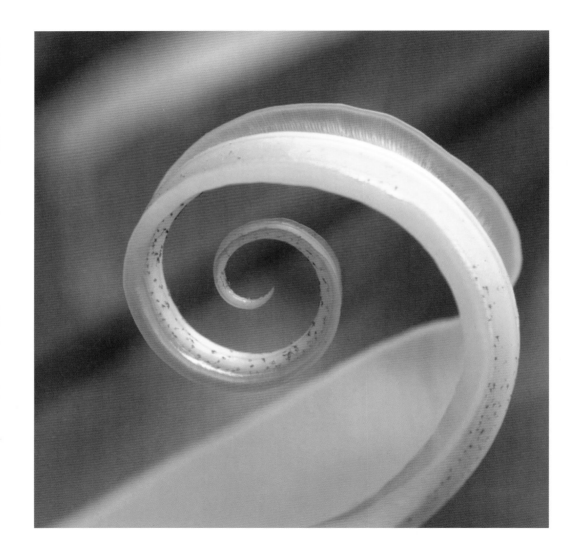

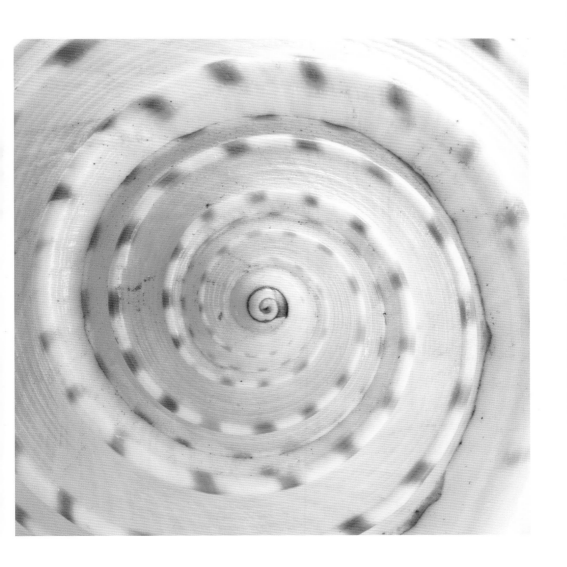

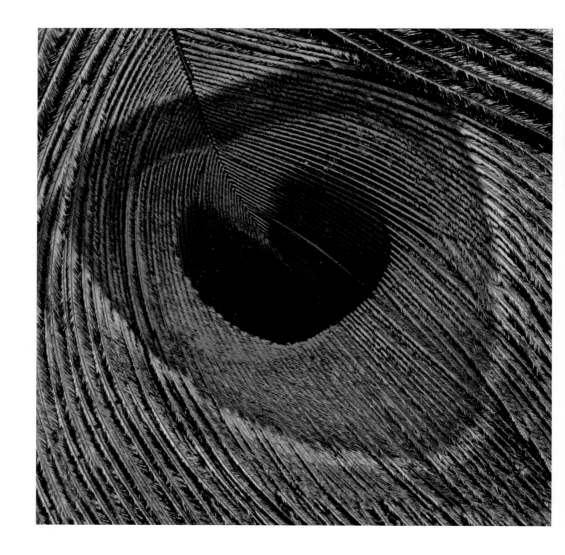

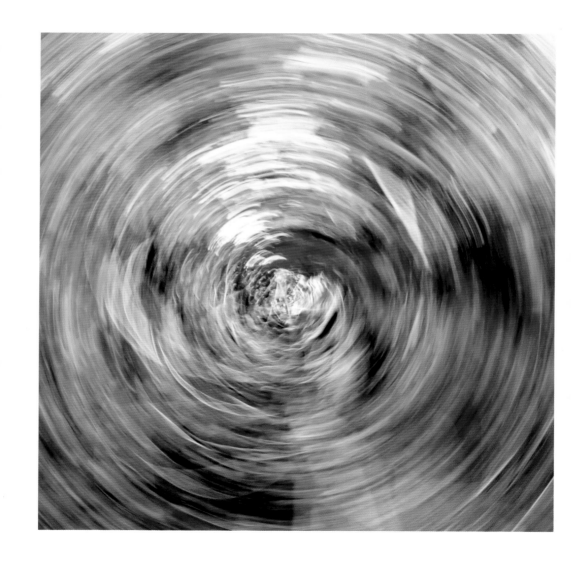

FURTHER READING

Bell, B. and Todd, D. *GaiaStar Mandalas: Ecstatic Visions of the Living Earth* Pomegranate Communications, Petaluna (USA), 2002

Brennan, B. and Smith, A. *Hands of Light: A Guide to Healing Through the Human Energy Field* Bantam Books Ltd, New York, 1990

Brownstein, A. *Extraordinary Healing: The Amazing Power of Your Body's Secret Healing System* Harbor Press Inc., Gig Harbor (USA), 2005

Chaitow, L. *Conquer Pain the Natural Way* Duncan Baird Publishers, London, 2007

Cole, J. *Ceremonies of the Seasons* Duncan Baird Publishers, London and New York, 2007

Cornell, J. *Mandala: Luminous Symbols for Healing* Quest Books, Wheaton (USA), 2006

Cornell, J. *The Mandala Healing Kit* Sounds True Audio, Louisville (USA), 2006

Cunningham, B. *Mandala: Journey to the Centre* Dorling Kindersley Publishing, New York, 2003

Dahlke, R. *Mandalas for Meditation* Sterling Publishing Company Inc., New York, 2002

Dahlke, R. *Mandalas of the World: A Meditating and Painting Guide* Sterling Publishing Company Inc., 2005

Mind, Body and Spirit Companion: Exercises and Meditations to Free Your Spirit and Fulfil Your Dreams Duncan Baird Publishers, London, and One Spirit, New York, 2006

Emoto, M. *The True Power of Water: Healing and Discovering Ourselves* Atria Books, New York, 2005

Fontana, D. *Learn to Meditate* Duncan Baird Publishers, London, and Chronicle Books, San Francisco, 1999

Fontana, D. *The Secret Language of Symbols* Duncan Baird Publishers, London, and Chronicle Books, San Francisco, 2003

Hageneder, F. *The Living Wisdom of Trees*, Duncan Baird Publishers, London 2005; Chronicle Books, San Francisco 2005

Hay, L. *You Can Heal Your Life* Hay House Inc., Carlsbad (USA), 2002

Hinz, Drs M. & J. *Learn to Balance Your Life* Duncan Baird Publishers, London, 2004

Huyser, A. *Mandala Workbook for Inner Self-Development* Binkey Kok Publications, Haarlem (NL), 2002

Levering, M. *Zen Inspirations* Duncan Baird Publishers, London, 2004

Levine, P. *Waking the Tiger: Healing Trauma – The Innate Capacity to Transform Overwhelming Experiences* North Atlantic Books, Berkeley (USA), 1997

McLeod, J. *Colours of the Soul: Transform Your Life Through Colour Therapy* O Books, Berkeley (USA), 2006

Parlett, S. *Crystal Meditation Kit* Duncan Baird Publishers, London, and Barnes and Noble, New York, 2005

Rose, E. M. & Dalto, A. R. *Create Your Own Sand Mandala Kit* Red Wheel Weiser, Newburyport (USA), 2004

Selby, A. *The Chakra Energy Plan* Duncan Baird Publishers, London and New York, 2006

Tucci, G. *The Theory and Practice of the Mandala* Dover Publications, Mineola (USA), 2001

Virtue, D. *Chakra Clearing: Awakening Your Spiritual Power to Know and Heal* (Book and CD) Hay House Inc., Carlsbad (USA), 2003

GENERAL INDEX

INDEX OF SYMBOLS

PICTURE CREDITS